Dance of
the Spirit

Dance of the Spirit

THE SEVEN STEPS OF WOMEN'S SPIRITUALITY

Maria Harris

BANTAM BOOKS
NEW YORK · TORONTO · LONDON · SYDNEY · AUCKLAND

DANCE OF THE SPIRIT
A Bantam Book / August 1989

Library of Congress Cataloging-in-Publication Data

Harris, Maria.
    Dance of the spirit : the seven steps of women's spirituality /
Maria Harris.
        p.   cm.
    Bibliography: p.
    Includes index.
    ISBN 0-553-05384-1
    1. Women—Religious life.   I. Title.
    BL625.7.H37   1989
291.4'082—dc20   89-6557
                                                          CIP

Published simultaneously in the United States and Canada

Bantam Books are published by Bantam Books, a division of
Bantam Doubleday Dell Publishing Group, Inc. Its trademark,
consisting of the words "Bantam Books" and the portrayal of a
rooster, is Registered in U.S. Patent and Trademark Office and in
other countries. Marca Registrada. Bantam Books, 666 Fifth Avenue, New York, New York 10103.

PRINTED IN THE UNITED STATES OF AMERICA
BP   0   9   8   7   6   5   4   3   2   1

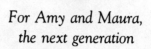

For Amy and Maura,
the next generation

Contents

Acknowledgments

My mother was a young widow. She lost her husband, my father, after ten brief years of marriage. It was a tragic loss, but in the changed household I had the positive experience of knowing the company of women in a special way. Her friends and co-workers, many of whom were women in similar circumstances, rallied round and supported her and us children with friendship, affection, and presence. Along with her, they gave me a wonderful array of role models and a fundamental awareness of women's spirituality as a thing of care and connection.

Years later, I was again strengthened and nurtured by a company of women, this time the Brentwood Sisters of Saint Joseph. First as their student, and then as one of their members throughout my early adulthood, I was once more gifted with role models and again tutored in a living spirituality. These women were and are intelligent, independent, and articulate about the spirit, on the one hand, and on the other, down-to-earth, witty, and wise. They taught me by the way they lived that spirituality is at the center of every day.

More recently, the company of women with whom I have explored spirituality has been my friends and colleagues. Friends like Joan Grace, Kathy Sperduto, Rosemary Crumlin, Gloria Durka, Barbara Gerlach, Joan McGinnis Knorr, Judy Dorney, Nancy Mann, and Jean Peterson have educated me in the many facets of women's spirituality and helped me clarify the themes in this book. And in crucial ways I can never repay, Joanmarie Smith, Barbara Masnick Rosenthal, and

Miriam Loretto Galasso have given me to myself, providing me with a music leading me into my own spirit's dance.

In shaping what I offer in this work, my gratitude begins with these women. But it must be directed to several other people too. First are my students. To some, I have seemed the role model (or so they tell me) and the instructor in spirituality. But they are models and teachers to me as well. I name especially Marg Blampied, Helen Bross, Kathryn Timpany, Kathleen Henry, Judith Keller, Blake Burnazos, Christina Braudaway-Baumann, Pat McCallum, Svea Fraser, Beverly Edwards, Rosemary Johnson, Helen Last, Marcia West, Katrina Clinton, and Peggy Howell for their specific contributions to the text. I thank Rosemary Cingari for helping me to understand the education of teenagers; Francis Tebbe for sharing his research on mentoring; and Ruth Baumann for her poetic descriptions of pregnancy and birth. To the New York University students in my Women and Spirituality class, I owe particular indebtedness for being with me in trial runs and saving me from dumb mistakes. Here I acknowledge Parvin Ahmadkhanlou, Linda Ende, Carol Briskin-Fuller, Chunk-ok Lee, Laura Lagerquist, Judy Pluta, Ellen Blum Cantos, Linda Rahn, and Esther-Okhee Choi.

I also wish to express particular thanks to Michelle Rapkin, my editor at Bantam, whose intelligence and counsel helped me write a much better book, and who saw me through drafts and revisions with patience and presence. I came away from each of our meetings with a sense of her reverence for me and the work that provided still another image of role modeling, as well as a living example of spirituality from a woman in the publishing world. Similarly, Assistant Editor Maria Mack helped me clarify and sharpen my writing with her understanding of what I was attempting to do and with her always astute questioning. I also honor the memory of Grace Bechtold, with whom I met too briefly because of her illness, but who encouraged and affirmed the acceptance of my work at Bantam.

I also thank my husband, Gabriel Moran, for the hour-by-hour and day-by-day support that nourishes my own spirituality and for the gentle, contemplative presence with which his love surrounds me. His quiet serenity makes the environment where I write one of ongoing peace, and his willingness to listen is a constant on both the good days and the not-so-good days.

Finally, to Freya Manston, my agent, who believed in me when I flagged in my belief in myself, who strengthened me with her professionalism, and who buoyed me up many times with her own great spirit, my deep, deep gratitude. Catalyst and counselor, sounding board and sister, she has always been there for me. I am indeed a most fortunate member of the blessed company of women.

Prologue

For almost two decades, as a teacher and educator, I have had the privilege of talking with women from around the world about a quiet revolution. That revolution is the rebirth of a genuine women's spirituality, which takes seriously the major issues in women's lives and the major elements in women's daily experience: issues such as brokenness, connection, and power; elements such as love, work, and death. As our conversations have progressed, I have become convinced that, although they touch us in different ways, certain themes are common to us all and certain questions are sedimented in our souls. And out of that conviction I have realized that the fundamental way of responding to these themes and questions is twofold.

First we must reshape and redesign the undersong of our lives—the *innerness* of our lives—according to a form and a framework that allows us to live the questions, love the questions, *dance* the questions. And *second*, we must pause, rest, and reflect, allowing ourselves the unhurried time brought by silence, prayer, and contemplation in order to help our spirituality flourish. In this prologue, I will describe the way I propose to help us do this by introducing the *framework* of the book, the *steps* in the Spirit's choreography, the Partner in our dance, and the *shape* of each chapter.

The Framework

As the basic foundation of this book, I present women's spirituality as a *Dance of the Spirit*; more specifically, as a series of steps. In order to get at the dynamisms in our spiritual lives, I propose that women's spirituality is a rhythmic series of movements, which, unlike the steps of a *ladder* or a *staircase*, do not go up and down. Instead the steps of *our* lives are much better imagined as steps in a dance, where there is movement backward and forward, turn and return, bending and bowing, circling and spiraling, and no need to finish or move on to the next step, except in our own good time, and God's. At whatever step we find ourselves, we are where we are meant to be. Leaning into and living into any one of the steps is the only way to understand it, and moving on to a next one happens according to our soul's own rhythm—in ways similar to the bodily rhythms natural to us as women.

The Steps

The sequence in this Dance of the Spirit has seven steps. The first, common to all spiritualities East and West, is *Awakening*—what one poet calls "coming to." That is followed by a looking around and seeing or noticing what is there *in* our spirituality—especially that which has been hidden until now, or only recently revealed. This is the step of *Dis-Covering*. And out of Dis-Covering then comes the impulse to take what we have found and gently mold our findings into a shape fitting for us in our time and in our world, bringing us into the step of *Creating*.

Once spirituality has taken shape and become formed, or *created*, it then becomes critical that we stay with it—and within it—for a while, that we "go apart and rest." This leads us into the step of *Dwelling*: an opportunity to let be and let go, as well as to come to terms with our livings and our dyings. Yet we are not long in Dwelling before we realize that to continue the movement in the rich and intense way we have lived it thus far demands those spiritual foods and "calisthenics of the soul," called *Nourishing* here, but in other spiritual teaching more commonly referred to as *disciplines*.

In some spiritualities, these five steps are the only ones offered. As primary caretakers of the next generation, however, women today experience a particular concern to *not* limit Spirituality to ourselves alone. Instead, an impulse lies deep within us to hand on to our daughters and sons the treasury of living which the dance of the spirit proves to be. And so a sixth step, *Traditioning*, claims us in the dance as essential to Spirituality, a step having to do with the ways those coming after us are educated into their own spirituality. And finally, in our own time and in our own world, the future's risks as well as its possibilities are so great that we are impelled beyond ourselves and our families to a spirituality that cares for the universe. That impetus brings us, finally, into a last step, *Transforming*, where our spirituality culminates in care for the entire cosmos. When that step is reached, we can stop for a while, but only to realize that we have reached the time to begin the dance once more, at a deeper, more fundamental level, in a never-ending rhythm of Awakening, Dis-Covering, Creating, Dwelling, Nourishing, Traditioning, and Transforming.

The Partner

This dance, however, is called the Dance of the Spirit. And this is a way of pointing out that throughout these seven steps we are not dancing alone, nor is the dance only of our own womanspirit. For as we are Awakening to the "more than" in our existence, Someone is Awakening to us. As we move into the deeper, further step of Dis-Covering and begin our care-filled searching, Something is seeking us, approaching us in return. As we create, a brooding, hovering, creative Presence touches us; as we attempt to Dwell in Mystery, the Beloved Spirit dwells in us. Nor do we do the Nourishing, or the Traditioning, or the Transforming on our own. For as we dance each of those last three steps, we realize that Someone or Something is Nourishing us, Traditioning us, Transforming us into becoming who we are called to be.

The Shape of Each Chapter

This is a book not only to read but to rest in. Therefore it is designed both as a movement through the steps, and as an abiding within each one. I compose each chapter in three parts in a format permitting us to do this. First there is a pause for Centering, where we sit quietly by ourselves, exploring the meaning the particular step has had in our lives until now. Second, there is the text or body of the chapter, where the particular step is described. And third, as each chapter concludes, seven practices or exercises are offered as ways of making the step not only one we read about, but one that we rest in and real-ize.

So, let us begin. In the company of one another, and of the Dancing Spirit, let us enter the world of our own depths, our own mystery, our own promise. Let us give ourselves time to wonder and to wait. Let us be patient and gentle with ourselves as we start. And let us believe that in doing so, we are contributing to our own wholeness and the wholeness of the world.

1
Awakening

A Pause for Centering

Let us begin by being still. Sit back in your spirit; you do that by sitting back in your body. This First Step in the Dance of the Spirit is Awakening, the Awakening of your Spirituality. Let your reflections on Awakening emerge from your inner self. Take time, don't hurry, and try to spend at least a few moments with each question, and with each of your responses, before going on to the next one.

> *When in your life do you find you are most awake?*

> *When are you least awake?*

> *Are there moments or times in your life when you feel called to be awake to life in a deeper way than you are now?*

> *To what in your life are you most awake?*

> *To whom?*

> *Are you awake to yourself, to the self you are in the deepest parts of your being?*

> *Are you awake to your inner life, as well as to your outer life?*

> *Are you awake to God? Do you ever feel that God is calling you to a fuller life, addressing you in a special way, speaking your name with love, with tenderness?*

Are you awake to the presence of Mystery in your life? To what is real, but somehow beyond explaining?

Do you ever feel yourself touched by this Mystery? Do you ever feel yourself reaching out in order to make that touch of Mystery happen more often?

Has an event in your life—of either great joy or great sorrow— ever been the source for your spirit's awakening?

Were you more awake to your inner life, your spirituality, when you were a child than you are now?

Do you ever wish you could be back in touch with your childhood sense of wonder, of awe, of spirituality?

Are you awake to other people, especially to their losses, their sufferings?

Are you awake to the voices of the earth, to the stars, the wind, the sound of the rain?

Are you awake to the possibility of being happy?

———————

Many of us take our waking slowly. We hold back, not wanting to go into the new day. It asks too much of us; makes too many demands. We are frightened; scared that we may lose the little we already have, the little we can call ours.

Others of us are still children in our waking. We anticipate each day as if it were our first—we feel shiny inside and outside. For us, no limits exist, and even if it is a dreary day, we feel ourselves surrounded by care.

Still others of us, all too often, wake abruptly. We are startled into the new day, shocked into it. Our systems aren't given time to adjust. We feel cheated—sleep and dreaming have been stolen from us too soon.

And then there are the Awakenings of anticipation. The days of being absolutely convinced that this is the day we start over and begin again. Literally, this is the day that God has made, the dawning of a time to rejoice and be glad. For today is the beginning of possibility, of fullness, and, finally, of happiness.

Whatever the circumstances, this coming out of sleep is familiar to everyone. Less familiar, however, is the *symbolism* this daily happening holds for a deeper and fuller Awakening. Less familiar, too, is the clue in each daily, bodily awakening which, if followed, can lead into new worlds. For people awaken not only *from* something; people awaken *to* and *toward* something. And the intimations of a budding spirituality begin when people awaken to themselves: to their deepest inner selves. It begins when people awaken to their sacred selves, and to God, to Mystery, and to the presence of the awesome in the world around them. It begins as people awaken consciously to the presence of sorrow and pity in the world as well as to joy and to delight. Or, to put it another way, people begin the dance of the spirit as they awaken to the possibility and glory of their spirituality. Today, throughout the world, as never before, this awakening is happening to women.

A woman who is seeking a richer spiritual life needs to probe the meaning of awakening in order to get a sense of it—to get a feeling for its texture, sound, and taste. And so this first chapter is an exploration of Awakening, the initial step in all spirituality. To understand Awakening, and to know how to move about within this first step, we have to study its choreography. So we need to attend to three themes: (1) the meanings of awakening in general and the teaching from both Western and Eastern religions concerning the awakening of spirituality; (2) the particular awakenings that contribute to the spirituality of women; and (3) those attitudes and approaches that can help us learn the moves of Awakening as part of our own spiritual dance.

Awakening:
A Recurring Theme
in Spirituality

Spiritual Awakening

The Awakening of spirituality resembles the awakening of poets and artists. Painters speak of the awakened eye, where seeing is complete, alert, and intense. Painters talk of facing paintings, and not only looking at them, but *feeling* them with their eyes. Artists acknowledge the awakening of the sense of touch in the hands and the fingertips, especially if they are potters or sculptors. Musicians, both performers and composers, know the awakening of the ear, the outer and the inner ear, to a special world of hearing. Dancers exult at the awakening of the entire body in movement, gesture, and rhythm. And those who are poets know the secret of awakening to words—to their sound and rhythm, their precision and splendor.

The Awakening of spirituality starts with this special form of *sensual* attentiveness, which all of us possess, to feeling, touching, seeing, and hearing, as well as to movement, gesture, and rhythm. As the Awakening of Spirituality begins, we gradually find ourselves becoming aware of the capacities and possibilities within ourselves to be sculptors, musicians, painters, and poets *of our spirituality*, able to hear, touch, and feel a new life emerging and blossoming from within. We find ourselves ready to become dancers—dancers of the spirit. We begin to look at things and people with more care, hearing words and music not heard before. We experience our senses coming alive, and we reach out to feel what we have not felt before. We move in new ways, with more assurance and more grace. We hold a leaf or a shell, a bird or a baby, as if for the very first time. We listen to a song or a symphony, a conversation or a cry, and feel ourselves stopping, pulled toward a response.

The Awakening which is the first step in all Spirituality starts here, but then it begins to build on this experience of the senses "coming to"—coming into their own and ready to receive everything in the universe. Although its point of departure is sometimes sudden, sometimes gradual, Awakening is nonetheless clear and obvious *attending*. It happens as a person begins to notice her characteristic ways of being-with, staying-in, resting, and listening as preliminary to whatever comes next. And with that comes another shift in the pattern: the experience of slowing down and taking time, just as in childhood, to wonder at how she is a part of the entire creation. These are moments of intense and poised standing still and listening in order to make a beginning. These are moments to be cherished.

Such Spiritual Awakening presumes a willingness to interact with and get to know, without haste, anxiety, or immediate results, the parts of our lives that are unseen. Spiritual Awakening is the capacity to start connecting with those aspects of ourselves that although real remain hidden—mystery, and love, and sorrow, and dreams of wholeness—those that make us truly *us*. Spiritual Awakening is unhurried, yet when people agree to step into it, and move around within it, it discloses magnificent possibilities—most importantly a movement toward discovery, creation, and transformation in the inner life. Layers, crusts, and shells which may have been built up over years become brittle, break apart, and begin to disappear. Muscles relax. And a realization dawns that a personal daystar has begun to shine, giving us its light.

The first step in the dance of the spirit, Spiritual Awakening, then begins in earnest. Something has made us alert and kindled our sensitivity to and awareness of the deep places, the quiet places, the hidden places. Something has called us to follow the hunch that now is the time to allow the light into these places, to be willing to look at the shadows too, and to become comfortable with both. Something has impelled us to befriend ourselves, one another, and the world in which we dwell. And although we recognize we are *claiming* our selves, sometimes for the first time, that *claim* is set in the midst of something greater, something more.

Western Spirituality

Western spiritual traditions place enormous stress on Awakening in the inner life. The Hebrew Bible is not only an appeal to awaken to ourselves, but also to the situation of the motherless child, the widow, and the defenseless poor. In that tradition as in most others Awakening is never totally private, never meant for an individual alone. Instead, it is always situated in community with others, especially communities of care. But, on the other hand, especially in the Psalms, the Hebrew Bible is also a call to awaken to a loving and attentive Mystery, always ready to receive us human beings; a Divine Listener who allows men and women to awaken in their own time; and Who is *there* when they do—aware of and alert to their needs. We can sink into that Divine Listener whenever we repeat the following verses from the Psalms:

> Now I can lie down and go to sleep and then awake,
> for Yahweh has hold of me. (Ps. 3:6)

> As soon as I lie down, I go quietly to sleep. You alone,
> my Strength, keep me perfectly safe. (Ps. 4:8)

> At dawn you hear my voice; at dawn I bring my plea
> expectantly before you. (Ps. 5:3)

And this daily comfort:

> I trust in you; in the morning remind me of your
> constant love. (Ps. 143:8)

In the New Testament, Awakening is also presented as a call from God, this time by John the Baptist, in preparing the way for the teaching of Jesus of Nazareth. "Awake!" shouts John, "and turn your life around. For the time of your deliverance is at hand." The call is even more evident in the Apostle Paul, who writes in his letter to the Romans words that continue to touch many today, as they reflect on choices that will either save or destroy the earth, choices related to world hunger and nuclear destruction and rape of the environment:

> You know what hour it is, how it is full time now for you to wake from sleep. The night is far gone; the day is at hand. (Rom. 13:11–12)

This Western teaching reaches a kind of centerpoint in the thirteenth and early fourteenth centuries when the great spiritual leader, Meister Eckhart, preached the core of the message on Awakening:

> *"This is Spirituality: Waking Up."*

In that teaching, Meister Eckhart called people to become responsible; to be alert in their senses to everything surrounding them, and to see fully with their eyes and hear fully with their ears. Thus having come alive, they could then learn to acknowledge creation as the great gift it is, and themselves at its center, dancing and singing the ancient words, "Glory, glory, glory; Holy, holy, holy." In doing that, they could break through to their own spirituality.

Eastern Spirituality

Awakening is a central theme and a core notion in Eastern spirituality as well. In Buddhism, for example, especially Zen Buddhism, Awakening is a kind of knowing that goes beyond possessing facts and data, beyond having information. In Eastern thought, Awakening is allied to that kind of artistic knowing named earlier. It teaches that when I say something like, "I see the tree and the tree sees me," I stop being a separate object and so does the tree, as if we were not connected to each other. Instead, we become partners: united, more whole than we were before, more aware of each other. Paradoxically, the awakening taught in the East is toward a person becoming more herself by allowing the tree to be more itself, and not merging or becoming absorbed into each other.

A seventeenth-century Chinese treatise on the art of painting makes this clear. In this guide, the artist is counseled to paint the picture in such a way that if she is painting a man looking at a mountain the man will appear to be bent in an attitude of homage and the mountain will appear to be bent in an attitude of acknowledgment. Or if a lutist is playing her instrument under the moon, the painter is advised to make it seem that the lutist is listening to the moon and the moon is listening to her.

Awakening in this sense gives life to everything, and by doing that, lets everything in creation be a companion and a source, returning life back to us. Everything is assumed capable of holding the sacred. When I am teaching spirituality I ask people to play with this connected awakening whenever they have the chance, sitting by the sea or a lake, for example, and allowing it to wash over their spirits, gently chanting: "I see the lake; the lake sees me." "I see the robins; the robins see me." "I see the stars; the stars see me." Or, in an urban context, "I see the traffic; the traffic sees me." "I feel the energy; the energy feels me."

Such attentive playing with the universe helps a beginner in the practice of spirituality to understand another directive sometimes given by mentors or spiritual directors to "Go out, and pray a flower." "Go out, and pray your childhood." "Go out, and pray the winter." The directive is a *koan* or puzzle, such as the one given by the Zen master asking, "What is the sound of one hand clapping?" or "What did your face look like before you were born?" It sharpens and alerts the spirit of the beginner to become awake to the Mystery of Being, and to enter its depths. And out of that work the beginner learns that she is always able to engage in praying—and playing—and dancing—the universe, whether it is a robin or traffic. And *careful* playing and praying and dancing then awakens her to the world of mystery everywhere. For these directions to pray and play and dance are, in the language of spirituality, directions which can be translated: "Wake up. Wake up to the lake, to the robins. Wake up to the traffic. Wake up to yourself, your childhood. Wake up to your spirituality. The time is at hand."

Such practices as these, in both Western and Eastern spiritualities, are directing women today to an attitude which, although forgotten in more recent times, is now being renewed; an attitude that makes alertness and awareness and awakening critical to spirituality. And as women recognize the presence of this attitude in themselves, they are turning to the next and more specific part of the first step—finding out what is special to the particular awakenings of women. Building on the universal meaning of awakening, we women are moving into those more personal parts of it which are enabling us to become who we are. These more personal aspects are *body, spirit,* and *crises.*

Awakenings in Women's Spirituality

As we have seen, Awakening begins with our senses and our bodiliness. Therefore, there is only one place to start: the body. Women's Awakening begins with attentiveness to the marvelous and wonderful creation which is woman's body. Too much spirituality from the past, both in the Eastern and the Western worlds, has taught withdrawal from and denial of the body, and even doing violence to the body. We find this, for example, in teachings that encourage us to deny sexual pleasure or to suffer abuse in silence almost as if to say, "If it hurts it's good!" Even more, much if not all spirituality is tainted with suggestions that women's bodies are a source of evil, a source of "temptation" into sin, embodied in the saying many of us learned from our mothers—and fathers—"It's always the woman's fault." Unfairly and cruelly, women in the past have been called "witch," "sorceress," "temptress," and "harlot" and in the present "bitch," "whore," "cunt," and "piece of ass." And often, "source of evil": not a source of evil for themselves, but for men and for society.

At times when women have been unreflective, or have not learned to love themselves first, they have, unfortunately, developed the truly terrible and terrorizing capacity for hating themselves and other women. Systems in society as a whole have put women in competition with one another—whether we are mother and daughter, co-workers, or doctor and patient—and then have taught us to blame one another—never the system—for our pain. Some women, more alert to what the negation and putting down of women has done in history, have shouted no, but until very recently these women have found themselves alone in their shouting, or exiled because of it. And so women, and men, need to engage in the ritual step of casting out—the religious term is *exorcising*—the demon of woman-hating from spirituality, the demon that denies the flesh and blood reality every woman is. The first move in this step of *Awakening* then becomes looking, as women, upon our own bodies, which is to say, looking upon our own *realities*, and saying, as God said in creating us, "This is Good!"

Learning to Love Ourselves: Body and Spirit

A Barbara Walters television special provides us with an example of how to do some of this self-celebration. The special was based around the notion from the movie entitled *10* that a woman's body and appearance could be rated on a scale of 1 to 10, with 10 equivalent to gorgeous, beautiful, perfect; a notion that some people found obscene and woman-denying to begin with. In the special, Barbara interviewed four women. The first three were well-known actresses including Bo Derek, the female star of *10*. When asked how she would rate herself, each of these women answered with an "8" or a "9" or "perhaps 9 ½," but none gave herself a perfect "10." But then in her final interview, Barbara asked Bette Midler, the fourth woman, to rate herself. Her response: "Me? I'm a 40!" In other words, she refused to accept the question or the original idea. She knew her own reality as a woman to be based on a totally different understanding of completeness than the measurements of her body or the texture of her skin.

The Spirituality of women awakens with the refusal to acknowledge insulting questions, or as in Bette Midler's case, turning them around so that we see ourselves as "40"—off the scale—unique and unrepeatable creations direct from the hands of God. Yet often, while admitting there is more to them than meets the eye, women do not take the time to develop that "more." Or—and it is amazing how prevalent this attitude continues to be—women do not deep down *like* themselves. We reject, resist, and rebel against the bodies we are. We are too old or too young, too fat or too thin, too tall or too short, too shy or too aggressive. Our hair is too straight or too curly. Our nose is too big or too small. We are always in need of fixing, reshaping, and redoing. Our dissatisfaction with our bodies infects us by lessening our positive recognition of the gifts that we are and the possibilities we might become. And of course we are directed this way every time we open a magazine or a newspaper, or watch a TV ad that pictures a "real" woman: tall, unblemished, and anorexically thin.

The Awakening of our spirituality demands, however, breaking away from this habitual putting ourselves down, and taking a good look, a good listen, and a new stance. Waking up means waking up to who and what is really there. For example, one woman I know says she has gotten into the habit whenever she passes a mirror of stopping and saying to herself, "Hello, Beautiful! You really are one terrific person." She says it is teaching her to see herself differently. Once we begin to have a caring appreciation, we begin to have a sense of just how special we are. Quite literally, we "come to our senses" and begin to cherish, welcome, and befriend ourselves. We also become attuned to the uniqueness in one another. We begin to wake up.

Special Times

A first, and perhaps surprising, time to practice this receptivity, this hospitality toward ourselves, is whenever we get our period, or for older women at the time of the new moon. I remember not having my period for about a year recently (menopause had set in) and then, at the suggestion of my gynecologist—a wise and sensitive woman—began taking medication whose side effects included a regular period. Telling my friend Judy about this, I said with both regret and annoyance, "I thought I was finished with all that!" Judy's response was a revelation—and an Awakening for me. She told me about the wise woman, Agnes Whistling Elk, who had taught an Anglo woman that the monthly arrival of a period is a great spiritual gift. It is a symbol from the Source of Life that all life is given to us not only for working time, but for waiting time. For resting time and Awakening time. Just as all dances have resting points, so too does all spirituality. When the moon changes each month, and we change in its company, we are being reminded to be still, to listen, and to rest in our bodies so that our spirituality will have time to flourish. Bleeding is a blessing. It is not, as too many of us were told *and found ourselves believing*, a curse.

Pregnancy and birth and nursing children are similar occasions for understanding our bodies and—if we take time—our spirituality. They teach us that genuine spirituality never turns away from engagement with life, from new beginnings, from food and nourishment, from caring for others. They teach us there are many forms of pregnancy and birthing and nursing as well. For example, it is possible to be pregnant with a dream, to bring forth a book or a poem, to nurture new life in a friend or in a daughter at the brink of womanhood. Powerful too in our spirituality is the practice of and delight in our sexuality, which like the beauty of a woman's body is a topic often left outside supportive teaching on spirituality. The budding and blossoming of our breasts in adolescence is a cause for celebration, not only for their shape and beauty and their symbolism of adult sexuality, but because they are reminders of the power women possess to be life givers. The physicality in making love is actually, ideally, a supreme moment of spirituality, a supreme moment for going out of ourselves—ecstasy meaning "outside of the self"—and all great mystics, describing meetings with the Divine, fall back on sexual images such as rapture or ecstasy or union or penetration. Indeed, one of the loveliest and most sexual books in the Bible is the Song of Songs, often taken as a description of the relation of the human being—body *and* spirit—with the Mystery Who is God.

And our task at the first step of Spirituality as we awaken to our own depths and heights, is learning to accept and love and awaken to our sexuality too, instead of going the way of denial and repression. Our task is to help our daughters also as they come into an understanding of their own gifts as women—a work we will attend to at length at the Sixth Step, Traditioning. For now, however, the task is acceptance, appreciation, and love of our own bodies. And the celebration of how *good* it is to be in a woman's body.

Spilling over into Spirit

If we can learn to love our bodies, we will find this attitude spilling over into our spirits. We will wake up as women to the essential connection between body and spirit, and come to know that the way to spirituality, and therefore the way to God and to everyone and everything else, is through the body. And in the connection, *never* in the separation, we will begin to cultivate a rich inner life. Once we become attuned to the companionship between our bodies and spirits, we will begin to see visions and to dream dreams. We will begin to realize that any moment is a moment when we might meet God; any place is a place we might meet God—or God might meet us. We will begin to realize that we can practice spirituality anywhere, anytime; that it is not a realm of life entered only on special occasions. We will begin to reclaim the mystical experiences that until now we had not recognized as times of intense spirituality: walking in the snow, swimming in the ocean or diving into its breakers, blowing out the candles on a birthday cake, holding the hand of our child; playing basketball or tennis or taking an exhilarating run, sharing a glass of wine or going to bed with someone we love deeply.

We will also begin to recognize ties with the women like ourselves who tell us their own stories of Awakening, and by doing so, help us to reclaim and tell ours too. Stories like these, of women suddenly drawn into the rhythms of waking up:

I was alone on a beach . . . early one morning in summer. There was no one else there, no houses in sight, and no boats passing.

I suddenly felt, in a way, disembodied—that the sea and the sky and the sand were all part of me as I was part of them, and at the same moment I felt that Time as we know it—a road on which we travel from the past through the present to the future—did not exist, but that past, present, and future were one so that thousands of years in the future were the same.

I had a sensation of extraordinary happiness.

Or this from a woman of sixty:

From the time I was a child I had occasionally what I now realize was a mystical experience. I particularly remember an occasion in my teens when I looked out of a window at a tree and knew that the tree and I were one. [Remember the earlier insight: "I see the tree; the tree sees me."] But instead of losing myself in the oneness . . . I seemed to be reaching an apprehension of what this signified.

Or this from a woman of forty-five:

I awoke in the middle of the night, still burdened with anxiety, and prayed, using the words of the hymn,
> Thou Whose almighty Word
> Chaos and darkness heard . . .
> Let there be light.
I lay in bed conscious of being absolutely wide awake. The bedroom seemed to be filled with an atmosphere of peace and light (though it was still dark) which was almost tangible.

Or this from a woman trying to interpret for herself the Awakenings of spirituality as she was coming to know them:

sometimes one's own effort, one's own need is operative, but equally the light breaks through when one's attention seems not to be turned in that direction at all. I think over and above all one simply comes to the conclusion that there is another reality, dimly seen for the most part as through a fog . . . or on occasion, revelation when there is a quality of light, warmth, and a new depth of understanding and joy over and above all.

"One simply comes to the conclusion that there is another reality . . . a quality of light, warmth, and . . . joy over and above all." That sentence could be spoken by any woman coming to a realization of her own spirituality. Facing the meaning of her entire experience, she starts to hear the echoes of a divine life within herself. She begins to be aware that Something or Someone—"another Reality"—is leading her into the dance.

Crucial Times

Although the Awakening of our Spirituality happens on its own time, happens from within and cannot be hurried—in the manner of the coming of spring or the birth of a child—certain experiences in our lives set the stage. Things happen to us or around us which shift the furnishing of our lives just enough to suggest a new pattern. Or, at other times and more dramatically, something completely reorients us in a new direction. Such occurrences signify *crucial times*. They can throw light on the Awakening of women's spirituality in general; they can also illuminate Awakening as it occurs to each of us personally.

In the language of psychology, these crucial times are often called *crises*. Some crises are dreadful ordeals: illness, accident, divorce, or tragic death. But not always. Just as often, a *crisis* can be a natural transition. The first day we went to school; our first period; our first time having intercourse; the first job we take after our children are grown are all critical events. An unexpected conversation can turn out to be a crisis, as can a momentary response of wonder, or a quiet walk on a summer evening. Birth—our own—is the first crisis, but learning to walk, learning to speak, learning to play the flute can also qualify as crucial. The onset of adolescence is a crisis with its terrible self-consciousness, weight-consciousness, body-consciousness. But so too is a first real romance or a first crush. Or going to college or getting married. So too are the times when the man next door falls in love with us or we tell our families we are lesbian or we adopt a child. Or we find a lump in our breast or our company decides to promote us or we bury a parent.

What all of these have in common is the presence of some kind of "marker"—some decisive, remembered event that rearranges our normal perceptions and patterns, enabling newness to break in. At a particular moment, we reach a point where increased vulnerability meets with deepened awareness. And that meeting precipitates Awakening to that Someone or Something that is impelling us—urging us—into entertaining a new perspective on life. With remarkable and stunning regularity, the Someone turns out to be God—not beyond the farthest planet—but deep inside. We may wake suddenly to finding God in ourselves, for example, and learning "to love her, to love her fiercely," as poet Ntozake Shange puts it. Or we may wake to the realization that we have been moved into finally telling ourselves the truths about our lives—many of us for the first time—*and* that it's all right.

Which means, finally, we are moving from silence to speech, to finding our own voices. For the first time in history, our voices, women's voices, are being recorded throughout the world, and over and over we are finding that the voices of other women are our voices too, saying our words. What has meaning for one of us turns out to have meaning for many of us. And as we are telling these truths about our lives, the world is splitting open to reveal untold surprise and mystery, as in these three discoveries women tell of themselves:

> You know, I always used to keep things inside because I would think it might be stupid or it wouldn't have any meaning and that nobody would care what I said. But now I can speak out.

or:

> I'm turning in. I try and watch myself more. Like if I had watched myself years ago, it would have been pretty boring because I really wasn't doing anything. I wasn't changing.

or:

> I keep discovering things inside myself. I am seeing myself all the time in a different light.

And hearing these voices, these accounts of Awakening, simple as they are, we hear our own voices too, responding, "I know that voice, and those words. They sound just like mine. And I thought I was alone."

Crucial times, then, to use religious language, are great *graces*. And they are essential at the first Step, that of Awakening, because they alert us to sources of new possibility, and perhaps more dramatically, sources of new power both within and around ourselves. They have a dynamic (*dynamis* is the Greek word for "power") which urges us on to further steps, like Dis-Covering and Creating. They may begin as a lump in our throat, or a sense of failure, or a longing for which we have no name. They may begin as a cry from deep within our soul. They may be precipitated by a searing, bloody argument with someone we thought we loved. But they have a way of seeping into us, rinsing through us, and changing the way we are and see and speak so that we can never be that earlier unseeing, unspeaking, unfeeling self again.

Attitudes and Approaches Toward Awakening

If Awakening happens from inside, on its own time, and cannot be programmed, hurried, or pushed, are we simply to wait for it? Or is there something we can do, if not to make it happen, at least to cultivate it, just as we might cultivate a garden? At the end of this chapter are a set of seven practices in this direction. Mostly they give us opportunities for becoming aware of the Awakening already going on within us. But in the meantime four attitudes and approaches can bring surprising results. We can remove our makeup. We can take off our shoes. We can stop believing in lies. And we can be willing to grow up.

Removing Our Makeup

Recently, I came across some pictures in an art book, pictures of women that had been painted by *women* artists. I was struck by the different way we see ourselves as women from the way male artists do—in paintings of nudes, for example, when women paint, the picture is far closer to what we see in the mirror. At least it seems so to me. There are bumps and blemishes, and surprisingly endearing imperfections. Women artists are able to paint—and have painted—the particular and poignant homeliness in all of our faces, without removing the beauty of those faces. It is from such experiences as this that I suggest the approach and attitude of taking off our makeup.

Possibly the suggestion that we take off our makeup, or go outside without it, creates a feeling close to panic. ("Oh God, no!") If we react that way, it may be we are shocked by the suggestion that we allow someone else to see us as we actually *are*. Just as it is difficult to awaken to the sound of our own voices, it may be difficult to awaken to the sight of our own faces. To claim them and cherish them and allow others to claim and cherish them too. I know. I wear makeup. But I marvel at women who go without it, and I notice how comfortable men are in public without it. And I wonder what our own doing away with it, not all the time but on occasion, as an experiment, might do in awakening our spirituality. After all, in *West Side Story*, Maria didn't sing, "I *look* pretty." She sang, "I *feel* pretty." (You women reading this who never wear makeup anymore, or who never wore it, or who don't need it because you are young and beautiful and know that, please don't smirk: stand there on the sidelines, instead, please, and root for the rest of us.)

Actually, the point of offering this as an approach to Awakening is to alert us to the many kinds of makeup we as women wear, and to our reasons for wearing it. It is the *symbolic* power of makeup that is really the issue. For cosmetics, which are probably the easiest masks to remove, are a symbol of all the masks we have learned to wear in public; masks that keep us not only from seeing ourselves, but also from *being* ourselves. Masks that keep us from our own aging or our own pain or our own beauty—or our own gaze.

A much more constricting and damaging mask is the false *expression* we so often wear: of peaceful agreement when we are in raging disagreement; of pleasure when we are actually disgusted; of distaste when we are actually delighted; of humor when we are actually repelled; of understanding when we are actually baffled. We are so out of touch with our own feelings sometimes, that we have learned to produce what we know is the *expected* feeling. We are so intent on pleasing others—especially men when they are bosses, husbands, or lovers, but other women too—that we learn to fake our reactions, and when we get really good at that, we learn to stop noticing our true ones. But Awakening is the step where we begin putting an end to masks, to pulling the covers back over our heads, to pretending. Awakening is the step where we start seeing ourselves in a new light. So a first approach is to take off all the kinds of makeup we customarily wear and find out what difference it makes in our sense of ourselves, and in the direction of our own lives. We may discover the shock of the experience helps to wake us up.

Taking Off Our Shoes

While taking off our makeup is probably something about which we initially may not feel good, the suggestion to take off our shoes is usually a welcome one. Many of us take off our shoes as soon as we come in the door, or slip into our Dr. Scholls, or wear sneakers whenever we can, having learned to *carry* our high heels, if indeed we still own them. Apparently, we do not mind what people think of our feet anywhere near as much as we care what they think of our faces.

But the meaning of this attitude, this approach here has to do with the ancient religious command that when you are in the presence of the Holy, you remove your shoes. The story of Moses in the Bible, for example, in becoming aware of the burning bush is one where Moses is suddenly awake to the presence of God in the bush, and at the same time is physically stunned into removing his sandals because he realizes he is standing on holy ground. And I suggest this as something that will further Awakening for us because we need to wake up to the reality that *all* ground is holy, and any place can be the place where we awaken to the presence of God. We need to awaken to the spirituality pulsing and growing its own life within us, and to the birth of our own dancing in the divine company.

In our imaginations, it helps to look forward to our day, or backward upon it in the evening, and try to remember all the people we have met and places we have been—and then to ask ourselves in what way our standing with them has been a standing on holy ground. It helps even more if, whenever we go into a room, or walk into a store, or say hello to another woman, or pick up a child, or have a meal with a friend, we remind ourselves that in this meeting, at this place, the sacred can be found. And when we begin to do that, we begin to awaken to spirituality as a reality surrounding us everywhere—a reality that is coming to meet us, even as we go in search of it. Still, some places will always strike us as special; for me it is the breakfast table with my husband; for my friend Ruth it is her baby's bath.

Stop Believing in Lies

Equally important, we need to start exercising the power of disbelief. One wise older woman, Elizabeth Janeway, tells us that those who are weak have two great powers: bonding and disbelief. I will say much more about bonding at other steps in the dance, especially the seventh, but in starting out, it is disbelief that is crucial. For it has the power to cultivate and foster Awakening, especially when we use it as an attitude where we face—and stare down—all the lies about ourselves we as women have been taught, and to which we have agreed.

These lies are familiar to most of us: That we are weak, while men are strong. That we are the heart in society, while others are the head. That we cannot appear to be too powerful or too smart or we'll either be told we're uppity or we'll "never get a man." That if we assert ourselves regularly we will be condemned to loneliness and no one will ever love us.

Even more devastating in many ways, because they go to the core of what it is to be human and in the image of God, are the *religious* lies we have been taught: That God is male, and so men just understand him (him?) better than women do. That if we need advice in our spiritual lives we must seek it from a priest or rabbi, rather than a mother or a friend. That women are not worthy to serve at the altar of God, even to touch it. That anything having to do with our sexuality is suspect, and that if we are menstruating it's best that we stay out of the temple altogether. That the first rule in spirituality is to deny ourselves. That sin was introduced into the world by a woman.

In response to these lies (and deep down within us we know they are lies), I propose the attitude of disbelief, for it will nurture Awakening. We do not have to argue our disbelief out loud, unless we want to; we do not have to go out and demonstrate our disbelief, unless we want to; we do not have to resign from our local temple or church or synagogue when it supports these positions, unless we want to.

But, if we want to take part in the full Awakening of the Spirituality to which we are called, if we want to take on our vocation to be bearers and birthers of the real God—the God who *is* God—then we must learn to practice *disbelief*. We can say it quietly or we can shout it. But when told we are inferior or unworthy *because we are women*, then we must say something. And in the face of the lies about our spiritual incapacities, there is only one thing to say. And it is "No, I don't believe that. Not any more." In such words reside the power of Awakening.

Be Willing to Grow Up

Growing up, like waking up, is often difficult and painful. Yet growing up and waking up are very closely related. I was taught long ago that in order to assess whether a person had really grown up, there were signs to watch for. These are also signs of Awakening. And the signs are that we suddenly wake up one day and find we have stopped saying these things: First, we no longer say, "Someone will always take care of me."

Second, we no longer say, "If I please them, they'll be nice to me." Third, we no longer say, "Life is simple." And lastly, we no longer say, "I am not responsible for any of the pain in the world." And the point is this:

If we are to take the steps that lead *to* our Awakening and *through* our Awakening as women, we will not please everyone. And so at this first step, we need to realize that in contrast to being pleased, many will be displeased and not nice to us anymore, because for the first time they are encountering us not as submissive little girls but as strong adult women. And that should awaken us.

Further, if we begin taking *care* of ourselves—really caring for and cherishing and loving ourselves—a similar thing may happen. People—whether parents or a husband or a boss—who have an investment in taking care of us, because it keeps us reliant upon them and *them* from growing up too, will have to look more carefully and more seriously at us and at themselves because the light of Awakening is shining in our lives. That light is illuminating the shadows and the hidden places in our relationships.

But most of all, if we start taking the truly adult point of view that life is not at all simple but is instead incredibly complex, *and we say so*; if we start taking the truly adult point of view that evil and pain and suffering *do* exist and we are responsible for acknowledging it in ourselves and the wider society, *and we start resisting it*, then we will come to realize that we have Awakened to the life that is in us and around us. We will have completed much of the work of this first step of spirituality, and with fresh, clean faces, be standing firmly on our own two feet. And we will be standing strong: alert and alive and Awakened to a new day, no longer believing the lies that kept us asleep, conscious of ourselves as adult women. We will find ourselves ready and eager and already moving on to a second step and learning what that next step, Dis-Covering, has to teach us—about ourselves, one another, our world, our God, and, the dance of our own spirits.

The Practice of Awakening

Ideally, the seven practices of Awakening are opportunities to enter into the mystery that is yourself. Ideally, you should practice at least one of them every morning, giving yourself a full fifteen or twenty minutes even if you must therefore awaken earlier than you now do. Engaged in consistently, they will become rituals in your life, rituals that have their own rhythms, allowing you to remember and to awaken. If you cannot do them in the morning, you need to choose some other time during the day where you can be sure of uninterrupted time, quiet time of your own. For each practice the preliminary steps are to:

• Sit comfortably and easily, in a quiet place if possible, but on a bus or a train if that is necessary.

• Shut out any outside noise by attentiveness to your inner self.

• Close your eyes and become attuned to your own breathing, to the rhythm and pace of your own breath. Be sure to spend at least sixty seconds coming to awareness of your breathing. For some practices, you will need to open your eyes after this first minute; for others, the closing of your eyes is essential. You will discover for yourself for which ones it is necessary.

At the end of fifteen or twenty minutes, take another sixty seconds to be attentive to your breath. Then gently and slowly open your eyes and conclude with either a spoken word such as "Good morning" or "Amen," or with a gesture to the Mystery within you as an act of thanksgiving.

At the end of each chapter, as here, seven practices follow. Although these practices are designed for a woman working alone, some women may want to do them together in a group. The point of doing them, always, is to find out what works best for you. So feel free to adapt them or revise them in any way that "fits." If there is more strength and support in doing them with others, go in that direction. If there is more strength in doing them alone, then do so. You are the one to decide.

Practice 1: Choosing a Mantra

Read the practice first. Then engage in the three preliminary steps.

A mantra is a short phrase that helps concentrate the spirit. It is repeated regularly and ideally has a rhythm of its own. Often people are given a mantra by a spiritual guide; at other times it is appropriate to choose your own. This morning, you are asked to choose one for yourself, a mantra you will repeat several times every hour. The time in the morning is an extended period of repetition; during the day, the repeating of the mantra enables you to recapture and reclaim the peace of your morning practice. Here are some possibilities:

> "Here I am, world; here I am, universe. Welcome me as I welcome myself."

> "The time is now; the place is here."

> "It is time for me to awaken from sleep."

> "This is *my* spirituality: waking up."

> "At dawn you hear my voice; at dawn I bring my plea expectantly before you."

And yours: _____

Practice 2: Celebrating the Crises of My Life

Read the practice first. Then engage in the three preliminary steps.

Reflect on your life as a whole up until this time. In your imagination, pick up your life as you would a bouquet of flowers. Now allow your life to fall into four parts (which will not necessarily be the same number of years; for example, if you are thirty-six, your life will probably not fall perfectly into nine-year periods).

1. For the first part of your life, choose one crisis or marker event of that time. If you wish, write it in the space below.

2. Dwell silently for a moment with the event, letting the feeling of it return to you.

3. To what did that crisis awaken you? In yourself? In others? In life?

4. Now, move to the three other parts of your life, and repeat the meditation.

Practice 3: Spiritual Experience*

Read the practice first. Then engage in the three preliminary steps.

For some people, the crises that lead to Awakening are crises in their religious lives, their spiritual lives. These questions are designed to probe your feelings in this area.

1. Have you ever had an experience you would call "religious" or "spiritual," or an experience of what you might call "God"?

2. Has it had any permanent effect or influence on your life?

3. Can you recall any particular moment or period when you had a feeling of awakening self-consciousness; of feeling yourself an individual person with a degree of freedom and responsibility? Can you remember if this was associated with any spiritual feelings or ideas?

4. Some people look back to childhood as having been clearer, more vivid, more revealing than later life, while other people see their early experiences as only the first steps in a process of gradual awakening, which comes to fullness only in adulthood or may not yet be complete. Do you fall into either of these two groups, or is there some quite different pattern in your life?

5. What meanings do your answers to these questions have for you? Do they tell you anything about your own Awakening?

*Adapted from a questionnaire of the Religious Experience Research Unit, Oxford, England.

Practice 4: A Room of One's Own

Read the practice first. Then engage in the three preliminary steps.

Virginia Woolf talks of the need to have a "room of one's own." During these twenty minutes, you are asked to decide upon yours.

1. Imagine, while your eyes remain closed, the room you choose. It can be an actual room, or one in your own fantasy. Imagine its size, its color, its texture. Imagine the sounds or the lack of them, the quiet or lack of it, the place where you are sitting or standing or lying. Imagine it clearly enough that you will be able to describe it in detail for yourself later in the day.

2. With a pencil and a plain piece of paper, draw the design of your room. Again, sketch it in detail, and if possible color it as well.

3. Choose at least one room you expect to be in during the day that could serve as a room of your own.

Practice 5: Awakening to the Who and What of God

Read the practice first. Then engage in the three preliminary steps.

The purpose of this practice is to be awake to the presence or absence of the divinity in your life. After you close your eyes, repeat several times, *very slowly*, the words of Ntozake Shange:

> i found god in myself
> and i loved her
> i loved her fiercely

Breathe the words in; breathe the words out. Repeat them at least ten or fifteen times.

Now sit with them; sit with them silently.

Are you aware of any awakenings these words provoke in yourself?

If you had to answer the question, "Where do you find God?" what would be your response?

If you had to answer the question, "Is God within yourself?" what would be your response?

Conclude with at least sixty seconds of silent breathing.

Practice 6: Praying Your Spirituality

Read the practice first. Then engage in the three preliminary steps.

One way of touching your spirituality is to "pray it." The way to do this is to engage in the following practice.

After closing your eyes and breathing rhythmically, allow your spirituality, wherever it is, and whatever it is like, to emerge from within your own depths. Be quiet and attentive to it. Listen to it. Use your senses to welcome it: your eyes . . . your ears . . . your nose . . . your taste . . . your touch. Have a gentle but intense conversation with it. Give it all the time it needs. What does it tell you about yourself? What does it contribute to your Awakening? Is it mainly from within you, or is it mainly from without? If your Spirituality were a person, how would you describe her? Or him? See if you can hear your spirituality speaking to you now.

Before opening your eyes, take a few moments to celebrate your spirituality. Then breathe silently for at least sixty seconds with your eyes closed. Then gently, open your eyes, and be awake to the world around you.

Practice 7: Coming to Our Senses

After closing your eyes, be aware of your eyes as they rest behind your eyelids. Feel them resting in their places. Imagine what they will be seeing during the coming day. Ask them to be with you, and to help you to see during the day what is really before you; ask them to help you see beneath the surfaces of people, the surfaces of things, the surfaces of events.

After closing your eyes, be aware of your ears resting at the sides of your head. Feel them silently in their places. Imagine what they will be hearing during the coming day. Ask them to be with you, and to help you to hear during the day what is really spoken; ask them to help you listen beneath the surfaces of words, the surfaces of sound, the surfaces of events.

After closing your eyes, be aware of your mouth, and of your tongue, your teeth, and the inside of your mouth. Feel them silently in their places. Imagine what they will be tasting during the coming day. Ask them, invite them to be with you, fully alive, and to help you to taste during the day whatever food and drink you receive as nourishment, as gift. Ask them to help you be unhurried in your eating and drinking. Ask them to be with you in your Awakening to the food and the fruits of the earth.

After closing your eyes, be aware of your nose, and of your nostrils, and the air coming in and being exhaled. Feel your nose as it gently breathes in and out. Become aware of whatever smells and scents are around you; accept both the attractive and the repulsive. Ask your nose and your sense of smell to be with you in awakening to odor, whether good or bad, and to the need for air, for oxygen, and for breaths of rest and relaxation during the day.

After closing your eyes, be aware of your fingertips, and of the soles of your feet. Feel the surface your fingertips are touching; feel the shoes or stockings surrounding your feet. Try to discover where else on the surface of your skin you are responding to the sense of touch; be aware of your dress or blouse on your shoulders, the belt at your waist. Invite your sense of touch to be with you during the day, to help you handle all things reverently and gently, especially the other human beings you touch. Take time to simply be in your skin for a few moments.

2

Dis-Covering

A Pause for Centering

Before we begin, sit back in your spirit. To do that, sit back in your body. Breathe gently and easily. The second step is Dis-Covering: both the act itself of dis-covering and then dis-covering the elements of your spirituality. Let your feelings well up from inside you. Be careful not to rush. Pause as you come to each of the following questions, and try to spend some moments simply sitting with dis-covering. Do the same thing with each of your responses.

> *What does dis-covering mean to you personally, and what has it already meant in your life?*
>
> *Up to now, what have been the two or three great discoveries of your life?*
>
> *Did they come suddenly, as surprises?*
>
> *Or did they creep up on you, quietly, over time?*
>
> *Did they permanently change your life in any way?*
>
> *What are you searching for most in your life now?*
>
> *How deep—how intense—is your searching?*
>
> *Who, if anyone, are you looking for?*
>
> *Are you looking for some deeper sense of yourself, a self you know is there, yet is now hidden?*

Are you afraid to search or be lured by search? Afraid of what you might discover or eager for what you might find?

When you have made a discovery that seemed important, did you delight in it for a while but then forget it? Or did it rearrange your perceptions and your dreams?

Have you ever felt that the work of dis-covering was something you had to do, almost as if you had no choice?

Do you have any hunches that a call is coming to you, indicating something you are yet to find in your life?

Are you searching for Community?

Are you searching for God?

Is God searching for you?

————————————

One of the best-known and most cherished works in all literature is Dante's *Divine Comedy*, the profound and poetic description of the journey of one human being from the edge of darkness to the threshold of unimaginable light. The opening lines of the poem describe a person in the middle of life, surrounded by a dark wood, having a sense that the path he was on, and which he thought was the "right" one, is lost. "*Nel mezzo del cammin di nostra vita,/Mi ritrovai per una selva oscura,/Che la diritta via era smarrita.*" "Midway this way of life we're bound upon,/I woke to find myself in a dark wood,/Where the right road was wholly lost and gone." And in the midst of that experience, he says, "*mi ritrovai*": I re-found myself; I came upon myself; I dis-covered myself.

The second step of the dance of the spirit is about that experience. Having moved through the process of *Awakening*, and danced to awareness within that step, we now come to this second one, where we spiral downward, inward, and then outward—often in complete stillness and with no perceptible movement—looking for what makes us uniquely *us*. We go searching for the special mosaics that form our spirituality, especially the pieces that have been neglected, lost, or left out. We know their absence has kept us from our own deepest reality, kept us in "a dark wood," "*una selva oscura.*" Dante's epic poem is pertinent here because that great literary journey, that walk, that *dance*, like ours, symbolizes the step of Dis-Covering. It is inward as well as outward; it is down as well as up; it is centered on spiritual quest; it promises light at the end.

In one way, the first and second steps of our dance seem alike, because it takes time for many of us to admit these are both actual steps in spirituality. Many women, for example, think of the first step, Awakening, as *preliminary* to living a spiritual life, something they have to go through as a prerequisite, rather than recognizing that once they have begun the movement in that step, they are engaged in spirituality. Others imagine that the turnings of Dis-Covering—*responding, searching, finding*, and *re-membering*—are only warm-ups, exercises they must do before their *real* spirituality begins. But the truth is that all the smaller movements within each step are clues telling us we are already inside the dance of the Spirit. Awakening and Dis-Covering *are* the spiritual life, and to awaken to the possibility of "more" is to have already touched "more"; to be searching for the Mystery is to have already come upon it.

In another way, the two steps are different. The first step, Awakening, was one where much if not most energy went into sitting up, standing up, and taking personal inventory. We let our bodies be our bodies, and our spirits be our spirits. We learned to wait at the critical moments. Now, however, we make a shift, moving to a more defined activity and movement. At the core of Dis-Covering, as the word suggests, is the consciousness and even the *work* of removing barriers, pushing curtains aside, bringing to light what has been in shadow, and looking long and deep at what we've found—a work of unveiling and revealing. At the core of Dis-Covering is the *recognition* of what has perhaps been partially glimpsed and yet remains hidden—from ourselves, and about ourselves. At the core of Dis-Covering is the crumbling of a false or narrow notion of ourselves and the emergence of the truth of our being.

At this step, we work consciously with *dabhar*—the Hebrew word for "creative energy." This new energy born from Awakening lies ready within us, waiting to be tapped. And the process of tapping it forms three moments: one where we *explore* the feeling, sense, taste, and texture of the step of Dis-covering itself; a second where we pause to *befriend* those discoveries we are making; and a third where we *incorporate* into our lives the paradoxical dynamics which make dis-covering possible. The rhythm of these three moments now guides our dance.

The First Moment:
Exploring Dis-Covering Itself

The step of Dis-Covering has its own choreography, moving rhythmically and in almost circular form. It generally begins not with a person's own activity but with that of someone or something else. Some women will experience this Other as a "voice" or a "presence," at the very least as a conviction. As one woman notes:

> I had just been jilted and could not feel that life held anything for me. I had no suicidal tendencies, but found myself walking in the middle of a busy road. A voice (or a "Voice") said to me quite distinctly, "Stella, Stella, go to the pavement," and I found myself there. Since then I have, I think, been able to be of help and of use in the world.

And another woman says:

> Although the room was dark and I was alone, I had an overwhelming feeling that I was not alone. Someone was there with me. So near that this *presence* seemed to completely enfold me. I was not afraid but very awed.

Other women will feel It as more concrete: a beloved and familiar person such as a parent or a child raising a question we had never before faced: a community to which we belong calling on a capacity—like organization—we did not know we possessed; a local or world event we found we could not deny—a Holocaust or a Hiroshima, a Selma, Alabama, or a South Africa. For still others, the something else will be immensely simple: a single "click" caused by reading a line of poetry or seeing a stranger crying on a train. But whatever the source, the common experience will be that a deepened sense of some reality "beyond" or outside enters a woman's life, and she *knows* herself "called" or "chosen."

Alternatively, a person can characterize her experience only vaguely, if at all, with a comment such as one woman made to me. As she put it, "Something is calling me, but I do not yet know what it is. It's not so much something I have to *do*, as something I have to *find*." What was occurring to that woman—and is continuing to occur to other women today—is the sense of a *lure*; the receiving of an invitation to enter a new realm; and the conviction it is time to start a journey that will lead to changing her life.

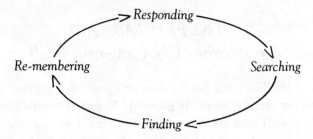

The Process of Dis-Covering

Responding

Dis-Covering only truly begins when one *responds* to the invitation and replies, "Here I am, I'm ready." Such a response will often demand great courage, for the invitation is never heard as superficial. The responding person knows she is hearing a call to move in a direction where everything in her life is up for grabs and open to new interpretation. Her experience is like that of Ruth in the Bible, who, when hearing that her mother-in-law, Naomi, is returning to her homeland, feels she *has to* accompany her, that something is calling her too. And even though someone—in this case, Naomi—tries to dissuade her, the answer Ruth gives is a classical example of this moment in the spirit's dance. "Don't ask me to change my mind," Ruth says. "This is a step I have to take. For somehow I know that wherever you go, I am to go. Wherever you dwell, I am to dwell. Your people are to be my people and your God my God. Where you die I will die and there I will be buried."

Searching

When the invitation is received and acknowledged, and a person responds to it, dis-covering then moves into a time of *searching*. People will often even speak of themselves now as seekers or searchers. "I'm a pilgrim," an older friend told me some years ago, "maybe a little further on than you are, but still a pilgrim." The form the searching can take will be as varied as we are. For some it will be in the joining of an organization, a church or a temple perhaps. For others it may take shape through going back to school or joining a self-help group such as an exercise class or Parents Without Partners. For still others, it may begin by deciding to start a love affair, or to engage in marriage counseling, or perhaps to divorce. In these circumstances, the searching will be done with other people, especially as we compare our own characteristic ways of living and doing and responding with theirs, exchanging ideas and advice. But the core of the work will be toward the dis-covering of a deeper "I" whom we know is present within us, and of a deeper world in which that "I" exists. And although the outward circumstances may seem mundane—like a change in our calendar or daily pattern for one hour a week—causing us to ask, "Is this spirituality?" the inward movement is often so enveloping and intense we have our answer.

In contrast, other searchers will go about the work of this step largely in solitude or with one other person such as a lover, a therapist, or a spiritual guide, much as Dante did in *The Divine Comedy*, first with Virgil and then with Beatrice. The work will be interior, with the other person acting not as teacher but as sounding board, listening to our accounts of whatever is happening to us.

And then there will be those who are searching alone, for whom a diary or a journal will often be the only exterior sign that something is going on in their lives. They will be like a Simone Weil or an Etty Hillesum, eventually leaving her writings behind for other searching women. Nevertheless, all these circumstances will have in common an active search for parts of herself that heretofore have been hidden or unknown, forgotten or forbidden. A woman will find herself asking age-old seekers' questions, wondering, "Why have I not noticed this until now?" or "Where did *that* come from?" or "What is this telling me about my life, my world, my future?" She will also find she is giving herself time, slowing down, and seeking to be unhurried in the quest.

Finding

Out of such involvement and questioning, if the Dis-Coverer remains open, she will eventually find her own voice saying, "Yes. That's the truth of things. That's what it's all about." She will find herself confirming original intuitions, perhaps at times standing quite still in worship before a gracious Divinity. She will begin experiencing moments of *unveiling* or *disclosure* or *revelation* which signal she is arriving at a new place, moving from the time of searching into the experience of *finding*. One woman says of this experience:

> Something woke me up. There was something or somebody
> by my bed . . . I think I had more peace then than I'd had
> for a very long time . . . I have enough knowledge to know
> that there's somebody there, to know that I need never be so
> alone again.

Such moments will often be quite brief—perhaps unattended—accompanied and characterized only by a swift sensation, a flashing shaft of sunlight or winter lightning, over before they've begun. Other moments of finding will be spun out, like long streams of colored time, enabling a person to savor them in their fullness, as in this experience:

> As I sat on a low wall opposite a beautiful tree covered with pink blossoms, thrown into a relief by the high hill behind it, I was suddenly made aware of my surroundings in a manner difficult to describe in words. The tree became vibrant, "real" (in the sense that the "burning bush" did to Moses) and I was transported into what I can only term "reality" and was filled with a great surge of joy—this was fundamental and I was "caught up into it" and *was part of it*. I felt a great sense of awe and reverence, permeated by the presence of a power that was completely real and in which I had my part to play. I knew that all was well and that all things were working together for good.

But whatever their length, these moments are landmarks for the person concerned, and enough for her to know she is in the presence of something other, something holy, something sacred. She is finding the "more-than," the "too-muchness" of existence, or even the "too-muchness" of God. And she is also catching glimpses of her own loveliness and her own value, her own power and her own gifts. She is catching glimpses, too, of the beauty and goodness and vulnerability existing in everything, in herself, and everyone else, and finding herself affirming hitherto-unknown aspects of the rest of reality—whether these are trees and lakes, tears and laughter, or the simple beauty of her own surroundings.

> I felt as though all the pieces in the mental jigsaw had suddenly fallen into place. I went home quite uplifted, and I remember our very ordinary little garden there, *looking quite different* . . . everything seemed clear and bright and joyful.

Re-Membering

And the natural result of such experience will generally be a movement and a desire in a woman toward integrating these unveilings into herself. She will find herself wanting to *re-member*. The remembering, however, will not be solely a mental act. Instead, it will be a re-membering or re-integrating of forgotten parts of herself into the present life she leads and the present person she is—much like folding beaten eggs into a sauce. The re-membering will be of aspects of herself that had become lost or dormant, like Elizabeth Barrett Browning's "childhood's faith" and "lost saints," or like the physical freedom of running or choral singing. The re-membering will be of forgotten people, of roots stemming from her grandmother and great-grandmother and those earlier foremothers, who will be claimed by the retelling of their stories. In time, she will dis-cover that the re-membering serves as the basis of the third step in spirituality, *Creating*. For now, however, she will rediscover herself ("*mi ritrovai*") in possession of an entire range of gifts, and she will move on to the new moment of exploring what she has found.

The Second Moment: Befriending the Discoveries

Because the step of Dis-Covering is experienced as unique and often as happening to us alone, it can come as a surprise that in all the great religions of the world, certain discoveries remain constant. Core elements that appear to be universal present themselves. Yet paradoxically, the one on the journey—or in this case, engaged in the dance—experiences the findings as met for the first time. For women today, this newness is particularly vivid, for although the pieces of the spirituality are as old as humanity, the dis-covering of women's spirituality in our time puts a new face upon them and lets them enter human life in a new way. And what are these universal dis-coveries that women on the path can expect to find? There are four: *brokenness, power, community,* and *divinity.*

The Dis-Covery of Brokenness

To move through the process of dis-covery with the wide-eyed vision of Awakening is to become aware, often for the first time, that something in our world is awry. It is not only ourselves who are out of joint or out of place—it is larger than that. In the truest sense, the stars too are out of joint, and the universe is at odds with itself. And the first great discovery that shapes our spirituality is one that all peoples before us have also come upon: the terrible conflict that rages in the universe between good and evil, life and death. This was the message of the fairy tales of our child-hood; even then we knew that dragons and monsters represented some-thing real, and that great forces were at war both in the heavens and in our hearts. Today, this is the message of the literature and art of our adult-hood, and often we discover our unconscious awareness of brokenness as impetus behind our original search. Our world rests on a fault line of tragedy, sorrow, and grief. Children suffer without cause; death comes without warning; and love evaporates, leaving no trace.

When we discover the pervasive character of brokenness and its mirroring within ourselves, a first response may be to deny it. A friend who has worked long and hard as an educator studying genocide tells of having visitors in her home one evening, and of her six-year-old daughter inno-cently asking them why they had numbers on their arms. She tells of her anguish in the moment, of her heart beating rapidly as a part of her said, "Oh no, not yet, I don't want her to know; she is too young to hear of the camps." But at another level, she realized she could not keep such terrible knowledge from her child—nor can any of us—because it is part of the human condition. We all walk in what one prayer calls a "valley of tears."

Acknowledging brokenness, however, is not the same as giving in to it. Instead, it is the way we honor the circumstances in which any spirituality we create will have to be forged. It means realizing at the beginning that although the world is one we cannot hold close enough for all its beauty, there are also pervasive tears in things—tears that alert us to the poignancy and precariousness of existence. In contrast to many spiritu-alities that speak of their goal as having a "clean heart," Native Americans describe spirituality as having a "moist heart," perhaps because native wisdom knows the soil of the human heart is necessarily watered with tears, and that tears keep the ground soft. From such ground new life is born.

In the context of this universal and cosmic brokenness, women today are discovering our own particular brokenness, with its own unique-ness. In the midst of a broken world, women are realizing that roles, expectations, and messages about themselves, received from the past, no longer fit. And so they face broken life patterns—whether these are patterns of work, job, marriage, and family life, or patterns of religious life, including women's images of God. And these broken patterns in turn affect women's relations with others, especially those closest to them, as they take on new roles. Those roles at the very least cause a "soft" bruising and at the very worst a searing pain. For one is not a mother or a wife or a daughter or a lover in the same way anymore, and new ways and attitudes are not yet clear. One is not a woman in business in the same way anymore, and new rules—if indeed there are some—are not yet clear. In the midst of these new patterns, the deepest brokenness begins to manifest itself, that within women themselves: emerging out of women's new desires and sense of self, in contrast to the desires they were taught to renounce and the false selves they were told to become. For one is not even a *woman* in the same way anymore.

The outcome of this is not despair, however, especially when a woman dances in the step of Dis-covering. Instead it is the dawning of a new wisdom. For beneath the brokenness lies a second discovery, critical to spirituality: the *power* residing within us to face and overcome the broken-ness. To paraphrase the Gospel of St. John, "A light is shining in the brokenness, and the brokenness is not able to master it."

The Dis-Covery of Power

When through response, searching, and finding a woman uncovers her own gifts and starts to re-member them, she begins to feel a new sense of power. She begins to see that her own gifts and her own powers are what will overcome darkness. She begins to realize not only that she *has* power, but that she is a repository of power—of a very specific set of powers. Unfortunately, many women have been brought up to think of power as a dirty word, perhaps even more so if they are religious women. They have been schooled in the notion that power corrupts. But for most women it is *powerlessness*, not power, that corrupts their lives and their dreams. And so the second dis-covery is that although pain and brokenness abound, grace abounds even more: the divinely bestowed grace of human and personal *power.*

At its root, power simply means *capacity* and *ability.* All human beings are naturally gifted with certain powers: to think, to love, to create, to be responsible. But in the act of unveiling the spirituality of today's women, it is possible to be very specific. For women possess a range of powers that are critical for ministering to the brokenness in ourselves and our world. Any searcher today encounters them too, and if she is wise, learns to befriend them. Chief among them are *vulnerability, emotion, caring,* and *connectedness.*

Vulnerability Ironically, a first discovery is that the capacity to be vulnerable, and to express weakness and even helplessness, is itself a power. To say to someone who has spoken to us brusquely, "That really hurt," or to admit out loud, "I can't do this alone," or "I'm feeling really anxious about this new baby," are expressions of strength. I say "ironically" because such admission is not usually thought of as a positive ability. On the contrary, vulnerability and weakness are feelings many of us are encouraged to dread and deny. Yet such feelings are common and inevitable to everyone, even though our tradition and culture may say only women feel them. More to the point, recognizing these feelings is actually a genuine strength, since being able to admit that as human beings we are regularly vulnerable, often weak, and many times helpless reveals a capacity for truth.

As women, we have learned to tolerate these feelings, and this toleration enables us to avoid wasting energy being defensive. We know, as Emily Dickinson knew, that pretending we are not at root vulnerable and in need is simply pretense: "Not to *discover* weakness is/The Artifice of Strength." The acknowledgment of weakness also makes it easier to go *beyond* the weakness, since naming something is usually the first step in dealing with it.

In the spiritual life, however, admitting we are often vulnerable and weak is essential, for this is the admission through which we express what is common to all human beings: our need for others and for God and our inability to go it alone. As W. H. Auden said, "We must love one another; we must love one another or die." The admission also serves to make us aware that even when they do not express it, all others—*including God*—need us in return. Through such awareness we begin bridging the brokenness between us and the rest of creation.

Emotion　As we continue our responding and searching, a second strength we find is the capacity to *accept* and *express* emotion. As with vulnerability, the assumption that this is a power is met by a long tradition of denial. Being "cool," *not* showing feeling, has been offered as an ideal, and women who are generally more expressive than men—we are given to crying in public without shame, for example—are often teased or belittled. Nonetheless, most women observing human situations, from staff or sales meetings at work to family conversations at home, have an intuitive sense of where feeling is entering in, what the feelings are, and whose feelings are being included or left out. We also know in our bones that being *unable* to feel—to "shut down" and cut off emotion—is one of the greatest losses a human being can experience.

What this enables us to contribute both to our own and others' spirituality is that in order for it to be complete, the heart must be included as well as the head. A spirituality strong in the head and *weak* in the heart is not spirituality at all. Religious gatherings, for example, that omit feeling or expression of emotion through avoiding music, physical movement, or the presence of children often feel strangely antiseptic to participants— except for those who have closed off their own emotions—precisely be- cause the only appeal made in them is an appeal to the intellect. Indeed, a religious service where a community gathers before God to express its deepest self may be the *last* place to keep a stiff upper lip or to "stay in control." For because it is human life, *spiritual* life must leave room for the expression of feeling, whether that expression is through the ecstatic singing of a communal "Hallelujah Chorus," or through the refusal to go gently into the good night of death, choosing instead to rage against the insulting intrusion of life's abrupt ending.

Caring   A third strength developed and demonstrated primarily in the lives of women is the power that comes in helping and caring for others. Most nurses are women; most attendants in nursing homes are women; most people who care for children are women. A fifty-year-old Bronx grandmother, living in poverty and raising two AIDS-infected grandchil- dren after her daughter's AIDS death, provides an example. Asked about her attitude toward the father of the children, a drug user now dying of AIDS, she responds, "I used to say I would seek revenge for what he did to my daughter. But . . . if he comes home to die, I will take care of him."

That woman, and others like her, demonstrate the *power* of care. For caring is not something that affects only the people cared for; it offers power and strength to the one caring. Care givers are taught about human relations through their caring—about the body's frailty, about the sudden- ness with which life's circumstances can change. Those who care about the very young know the swiftness of human growth; those who care for the very old know the inevitability of human decline. Caretakers have fewer illusions about the two greatest religious realities—birth and death—than those who have not been schooled by Care. They also provide a critical challenge to a society that makes idols of achievement and success, and suggests in the process that anyone who is nonproductive or unsuccessful—by society's standards—is somehow inferior. Caretakers remind the rest of us that each of our lives is an interplay of life and death, succeeding and failing, growing and declining. Even if they do not know the story, they carry in their bodies the wisdom of the following Myth of Care.

Care, it is said, was walking along the river one day, picking up earth and thinking, "Wouldn't it be wonderful if there could be human beings." But because Care couldn't *make* human beings, didn't have *that* power, Care asked God to take the earth and breathe life into it. And God did. Then and there it was decided that since God had breathed life into human beings, God would receive them when they died; God was where they were going. Because they were made from the earth, from the *humus*, they would be called "human." But because Care had thought of them in the first place, She would possess them all their lives.

Connectedness Finally, in our dis-covering, we inevitably come upon the central human power of *connection*, central because we now know it as essential to understanding ourselves as women. Two scholars, Carol Gilligan and Nancy Chodorow, shed invaluable light on all our lives here. Both women work from the discovery that women's development and maturity is located in our experience of relationships. Since it is usually true that for both sexes the primary caretaker in the first years of life is female, daughters more than sons tend to experience themselves as more like, and more continuous with this primary other who reflects themselves. ("A son is a son till he takes him a wife, but a daughter's a daughter the whole of her life" goes the folk saying.) The result is that as girls come to understand themselves as possessing female identity, they come to know themselves as *connected, related, at-one-with*. In contrast, boys coming to understand themselves as possessing male identity, come to know themselves as *separated, individual, autonomous*. The meaning of these differences has great impact on our self-understanding and on our inner life. Simply put, we as women *know ourselves* through attachment and connection. For us, separation is a threat. Men, in contrast, know themselves as they withdraw and become separate. For them, intimacy and attachment are threats.

As spirituality develops, especially when moral choices are made, judgments made by men are more often tied to the ability to decide on the basis of abstract principles, and not from connection and relations. Asked whether to save his dying wife a man should steal a drug from a druggist who owns it but is unwilling to sell it, men will typically say, "Yes, he should steal it, because saving a life is a higher principle than private ownership," whereas a woman will typically say, "Why doesn't he just sit down and talk with the druggist and explain the situation?" For judgments we make as women are generally tied to our power to empathize with other people and are embedded in relations.

This is closely related to a major barrier to a genuine women's spirituality in the past: the presentation of spirituality as synonymous with withdrawal from the world, with separating ourselves from what we love, and with severing connections—a situation intolerable to most women. This illuminates the discovery that any spirituality appropriate to us must incorporate our relations and connections, because it is these things that are central to our identity. We are not only ourselves, we are our relations, and the more related we are the better. Such a discovery as this, linked to our powers of *vulnerability, emotion,* and *care,* can enable us to claim what is uniquely ours. In addition, it can assist those men who are ready for a similar step. And because it refuses to sever connection it can empower the growing confidence that *our* searching and finding contributes to healing the brokenness of our world.

The Dis-Covery of Community

Brokenness and the awareness of our powers to respond to it remain incomplete dis-coveries without the presence of a third element. This is the revelation, born out of the power of connectedness, that we are part of everyone and everything that exists. Our call is to Community. True, our experience as we begin Dis-Covering is of a solitary spiraling down into a deep well. But when we touch bottom, the experience turns out to be that the waters of life and spirit underneath each of our own wells are common waters where all that has divided us begins to merge. In the merging, we dis-cover the impulse toward community.

The Western world was long cursed by the moment back in the sixteenth century when the wretched teaching was put forward that spirituality had to do only with the individual and God. However, our time is now being blessed with the re-discovery that Community as an essential element in spirituality has roots everywhere. Religiously, one of the strongest roots is the commandment to love each other as we love ourselves; a law just as gravity is a law, revealing what we are called to be. *To be,* here, means *to-be-with.* Another root is mysticism, the spiritual conviction found in all religions, that everyone and everything is related to everything and everyone else; that we are sisters and brothers to one another, despite differing races, religions, and nationalities. Mysticism also teaches that we are related to the other animals who share the Earth with us: cats and dogs, whales and whipporwills; and that we are also in community with the Earth's elements, with wind, water, fire, and soil. As our great foremother Mechtild of Magdeburg knew, "The truly wise person kneels at the feet of all creatures."

Nevertheless, as women re-membering community and blending it into our own spirituality, three of its facets are critical. The first is community within ourselves. We need to cultivate and cherish our deepest selves, drawing on the powers we have already named and adding to them others such as a quiet affirmation of our spiritual possibility and a wholesome gentleness toward our spiritual poverty. We need to learn how to be content and at home in our own company, and to take time alone, in a room of our own, to honor what Virginia Woolf called the "nuptials" of our spiritual life. "Not a wheel must grate, not a light glimmer. The curtains must be close drawn" so that in mind and spirit, we "might celebrate [our] nuptials in darkness." Otherwise, loving each other *as we love ourselves* may be difficult to do.

Second, we need to develop community with other women—especially with women of spiritual insight—whom we may not have listened to up to now. Among these are women of our own and other religions whose attitudes toward God are different from our own, and who because of that can give us fresh entry into the reality of God. Not only will these include women of the great world faiths (in one of my spirituality classes, for example, this means Buddhist, Muslim, Jewish, Protestant, and Catholic women coming together regularly), but those who are creating new religious forms or reinstating forgotten ones, such as worship of the Goddess.

The other women with whom we must find community are the women of the past: the female ancestors of our personal bloodlines, and the female ancestors in the human bloodline whose names are only now coming into the light. Christian women like the mystics Hildegard of Bingen and Julian of Norwich, who combined spirituality with the tensions of every day—Hildegard in the twelfth and Julian in the fourteenth century; Jewish women like the second-century Talmudic scholar Beruriah and the twentieth-century Bertha Pappenheim, who led German-Jewish feminism for twenty years; the Goddesses of African religion like Yemanja, Mawu, and Ala, who are revered as mother, creator, and provider of life. We need to search for community not only in our mothers' gardens but in those of our sisters and our cousins, our aunts and our great-aunts. And in reclaiming them into community with us we can begin to break down the great barriers to community in women's spirituality where women are set against women. Perhaps we can even reunite Sara with Hagar, Esther with Vashti, and Medusa with Athena. In doing so, we can end the tragic myth of woman as woman's enemy and create the kind of community where unnumbered women now dead are re-membered once more in our singing and our dancing.

And the third essential aspect of community will come in our sisterhood with Earth. The awesome danger in which our planet exists comes from weapons and from environmental pollution, of course. But this in turn comes from our unthinking collusion with attitudes and systems that poison Earth daily and hourly, rather than reverencing her as mother and as sister. Attitudes such as domination and acquisitiveness; systems such as unthinking militarism and unnecessary consumption. For a healthy spirituality, we must bring back into consciousness what we should never have forgotten: that the Earth does not belong to us, we belong to Earth; that we are part of the Earth and it is part of us. We can remember this whenever we pray with the Native American this prayer to the grass: "Let me so walk upon you, that even though you must bend your head under me as I pass by, you will know after I have gone that I am your sister." That is at least one way to remind ourselves we and Earth are destined to live in community together.

The Dis-Covery of Divinity

The last of our dis-coveries is not the fourth in a sequence, following *brokenness, power,* and *community.* Actually, it is not the *last* discovery at all, nor is it the first: It is both, and it is all those in between and all those yet to come. For we do not first discover brokenness, and then power, and then community, and then God. Spirituality does not work that way. Instead, as we discover the first three, we come upon the wisdom that the Holy Mystery who is named God—yet is ultimately Unnameable—is found in the midst of all our other discoveries. We come to the wisdom that divinity is at the center of brokenness, power, and community; and that God is not one more discovery on the list. Instead, God is in the Brokenness of brokenness, in the Power of power, in the Community of community. God is the Identity of our identity, the Spirituality of our spirituality.

In this dis-covering, we come upon a truth that is meant to sustain us throughout our spirituality—the truth that God is not a separate "object" or thing as other elements in existence are. Instead, as all great religious figures and mystics have taught, and as the necessary completion of mysticism itself, everything and everyone is related to everything and everyone else because God is within each and all of them. God is essentially the one who is "with"; even more, God *is* withness; God *is* with-in-ness.

> Julian of Norwich: We are in God, and God
> whom we do not see, is in us.

> Mechtild of Magdeburg: The day of my
> spiritual awakening was the day I saw—
> and knew I saw—all things in God and God
> in all things.

> Psalm 139: 8–10: If I climb the heavens,
> you are there: there too if I lie in shoel.
> If I flew to the point of sunrise
> or westward to the sea, Your hand would
> still be guiding me,
> your right hand, holding me.

> *The Divine Comedy:* The Primal Light the whole irradiates . . .

This discovery that God is as close to us as water in a sponge, or that God is in our body's veins and arteries as well as in the veins and arteries of our lives, is the fundamental music accompanying the entire dance of the spirit. "Every day is a god, each day is a god," sings Annie Dillard. "I wake in a god. I wake in arms holding my quilt, holding me as best they can inside my quilt." Through every movement and every gesture, every turn and return, every leap forward and every silent rest, the music remains— not only beneath but over and under and next to and within, just as God is beneath and over and under and next to and within. In the trees and in the lakes, in the laughter and in the tears, in the animals and in the sun, in the soil and the fire and the air and the water. In the lure and the invitation. In the responding, the searching, the finding, and the re-membering. And in every one of us.

The Third Moment:
Incorporating the Dynamics

Dis-covering is a natural process, which happens in any life when a person refuses to put obstacles in the way or works at removing them. Just as it did in the step of Awakening, the naturalness means we cannot *make* Dis-Covering happen on some set schedule. Still, each person possesses a set of dynamics within herself which she can draw on whenever she permits herself to enter the step of Dis-Covering. Each of these dynamics is a secret paradox, the secret being that if we hold on to both parts of the paradox *at the same time*, we will open ourselves to the call to be the permanent searchers all spirituality demands. The dynamics will enable us to make Dis-Covering a facet of our identity, and to incorporate into our lives the permanent realization there is always something more to be found. These dynamics are: (1) conviction and not-knowing, (2) balance and dis-equilibrium, (3) receptivity and refusal, and (4) holding on and letting go.

Conviction and Not-Knowing

Dis-Covering arises out of the *conviction that something is there to be found.* The energy underneath the process we have been describing is a rock-bottom realization that something is missing for us, but nevertheless exists in the universe, and we are called to search it out. In the search of spirituality, the conviction takes several forms.

One is the certainty there is indeed a spiritual realm—a world of meaning and wisdom and truth that is not immediately tangible. The presence of this conviction in the midst of a world whose technology is unsurpassed has particular importance today, because it signals a disillusionment in people: with the limits of a scientific world, with the scramble to the top, with show and glitter and glitz. In its place is a quiet but growing acceptance of the conviction that not everything can be said, or scientifically proven, and that the great realities of human life—love and death and sexuality and sorrow, fidelity, hope, and the awesome quest for peace—are what make us fundamentally human. Allied to this conviction is the realization that we have become diminished through dismissing this realm. Our personal salvation, as well as our salvation as a human people, depends upon our reclaiming it.

As we acknowledge these convictions, we realize that spirituality in our own times must be broadened and enriched by taking *our* lives seriously. It must also draw on the strengths that are manifested in the lives of women; it must be anchored, as women are, in the rhythms and steps of our bodies and our blood. The spirituality must be of the mothers and the daughters as well as of the fathers and the sons—leading perhaps to a new heaven and new earth where despair and war no longer exist, and all peoples are one.

And yet, although we know something is missing and awaits our finding it, we never know exactly what it is. This points to the other side of this dynamic: *not-knowing*. At one level we aren't certain where to look, and we realize we must be ready for failure and loss. We find ourselves willing and ready to admit that this was a wrong turn or a poor lead. And this means we need to retrace our steps. But much more critically, not-knowing feels right.

For at a deeper level, not-knowing is *itself* a crucial discovery of another *kind* of knowing. Not-knowing is not the same as being ignorant or as knowing nothing. Instead, it is a meeting with the puzzling truth embedded in all spirituality that we will *never* know completely what we have found. There will always be a sense of "more," because of the divinity residing in all reality. Always, when spiritual insight and understanding are genuine, we will dis-cover ourselves touched, shrouded, and veiled by Mystery.

Mystery means not that we cannot know *anything*; Mystery means that we cannot know *everything*—such as how a rose could come to be as it is. Or what makes our infant daughter smile at us as she does. The not-knowing in Spirituality signals the amazing security and strength we feel when journeying into a "Cloud of Unknowing" which has always partially concealed the most sacred moments of life: those of deep sorrow, sheer delight, intense love, stark terror, or ecstatic communion with God.

Balance and Dis-equilibrium

The second paradoxical pair fueling our dis-covering are balance and imbalance. On one hand, dis-covering is exhilarating and healthy, and it causes us to feel more whole, more sane, more *balanced* than we have ever felt in our lives. But at the same time, we also become aware there is a dis-equilibrium, an *imbalance*, deep inside us, almost a feeling of physical discomfort. The disequilibrium tends to arise from the feeling that the experience we have been living is not our own, and that unless we do our own dis-covering, the experience we have will be false or phony. We have the intense feeling that we no longer measure up. This time, however, it is not the unease of no longer meeting another's expectations, but rather it is the feeling we are not meeting our *own* sense of who we really are. Actually what is happening is that the powers within us are pushing us toward personal wholeness and away from a position of incompleteness caused by living someone else's idea of what we should be. These include our parents, whose image of the perfect daughter may have kept us from finding our own ("a good daughter calls her parents at least once a day"), our religious community, whose image of the perfect *person* may have done the same thing ("a good member of this community always dates her own kind"), or ourselves, wedded to an outmoded vision of what we ought to be. And so we find ourselves off-balance and shaken, often severely, by the realization that until now, in order to create the *appearance* of wholeness, we have rejected much of our own truth, and have been living someone else's.

Receptivity and Refusal

The movement toward equilibrium leads to a further dynamic where we become our own monitors and guides to what we take in and receive. We begin practicing a receptivity born out of many of the dis-coveries we have already noted: a receptivity to ourselves, other women, and the earth that we had never practiced before. We say to our souls, regularly, "Be still," and "Wait as long as you need," inspired by a new hope that we shall hear our personal call when it is spoken.

And yet simultaneously with this, we also practice refusal. We become skeptics of the spirit, slow to accept what we are told by others, especially when it does not harmonize with our own experience. We echo Edna St. Vincent Millay in this, who wrote once of her refusal to accept death, despite evidence, and gave us the mantra, "I am not resigned."

We begin saying no to people and invitations we would once have accepted immediately if they are not in harmony with our own wisdom and intuition. We find ourselves resisting interpretations that do not fit our music. We refuse to let ourselves die, or to bury ourselves, and in that refusal we dis-cover that we are continuing to become more complete.

Holding On and Letting Go

And finally in the step of Dis-Covering, we come to cherish two attitudes which are inseparable from each other and are a completing and resting point within this step. The first, *Holding On*, is needed because on one hand the step of Dis-Covering, especially as the searching and re-membering continues, can shake us badly. For as we dis-cover our lives, we realize we must create them anew. When that happens, the feeling may be of falling from a cliff or a high place, and of literally grasping with our fingernails. Dizziness and vertigo can threaten to engulf us. And so the dynamic of *Holding On* becomes our deeper self saying, "Don't let go; don't give up the responding, the searching, the finding, the re-membering. Hold on even when your arms ache and your back bends and the sweat runs down your face and you feel completely alone."

But at the same time, and paradoxically, the step of Dis-Covering is always a *Letting Go*. A letting go arising from the simplicity "costing no less than everything" where we stop cluttering our lives with trivia. A painful yet renewing letting go of old images and old formulas, as well as a letting go of old practices and outmoded beliefs. A letting go, as all spirituality eventually demands at some point, of the old self and putting on the new woman whose face we keep glimpsing along the path, who will lead us into the important next step of Creating. The woman who is our own true self.

The Practice
of Dis-Covering

Ideally, the seven practices of Dis-Covering are opportunities to dis-cover more about the mystery that you yourself are, and to dis-cover more about the mysteries that surround you. Ideally, you should practice at least one of them every day, giving yourself a full complement of fifteen or twenty minutes (which may be divided into parts), even if you must therefore rearrange your day. Engaged in consistently, they will become rituals in your life, rituals that have their own rhythms and allow and assist you in Dis-Covering, making this step a permanent part of your spirituality. The preliminary steps for each practice are to:

your sense of touch during the day to help you discover the things and people you will contact today?

At the end of fifteen or twenty minutes, take another sixty seconds to be attentive to your breath. Then gently and slowly open your eyes and conclude with either a spoken word such as "Good morning" or "Amen," or with a gesture to the mystery within you as an act of thanksgiving.

Practice 2: Dis-Covering the Women in Your Bloodline

Read the practice first. Then engage in the three preliminary steps.

Divide your life into ten-year periods.

For each period, choose two women who enabled you to develop as a human being.

As you reflect on each woman, describe her to yourself.

Imagine yourself as you are now, having a conversation with her.

> What do you want to tell her?
>
> What do you want to ask her?
>
> What does she want to tell you?
>
> What does she want to ask you?

Take the time not only to speak, in your imagination, but also to listen.

Conclude this practice by closing your eyes and celebrating the lives of these women.

Plan to do this practice some time in the future with a group of women friends.

Practice 3: Breathing in Divinity

Read the practice first. Then engage in the three preliminary steps.

In this chapter, we read of the dis-covery of God, or Divinity, as being present within everything that exists.

This is a mantra practice (see Practice 1 on p. 50); the mantra is "I am breathing in the Mystery of God."*

With your eyes closed, breathe silently for five minutes. Concentrate solely on your breath coming in, going out. For three seconds inhale; for three seconds exhale. Repeat.

After five minutes, as you take in each breath, repeat silently and gently, "I am breathing in the Mystery of God." Repeat the phrase on each breath for the next five minutes.

When these five minutes are over, move to the phrase, "I am breathing Mystery" on each breath. Repeat the phrase for five minutes.

When these five minutes are over, return to the practice of breathing silently and gently, without a word, for the last five minutes.

Without hurry, open your eyes.

---

*You may want to substitute a phrase such as "I am breathing in my Mother God," or "I am breathing in a new divinity," or one of your own choice.

Practice 4: Drawing Connections

Read the practice first. You will need a pencil and paper. Then engage in the three preliminary steps.

The work of this practice is to do exactly what it says: draw.

Begin by reading the following:

> One day on the road to Norwood, I noticed a bit of ivy round a thorn stem . . . and proceeded to make a pencil study of it in my gray paper pocket book, carefully, liking it more and more as I drew. When it was done, I saw that I had virtually lost all my time since I was twelve years old, because no one had ever told me to draw what was really there . . . I had never seen the beauty of anything, not even of a stone—how much less of a leaf.
>
> —John Ruskin

Now, go outside and find one piece of the nonhuman earth: a leaf, a stone, a piece of grass, a stick, anything. Take at least fifteen minutes to sit with it, to look at it, to see it, and finally to draw it.

Complete the practice by sitting silently with the object.

Practice 5: Dis-Covering Our Foremothers

Read the practice first. Then engage in the three preliminary steps. You may find you want to do this exercise with others.

This practice is different from some you have done thus far, because in it, you must do something after the twenty minutes of stillness.

But first, begin by remembering everything you know about each of your grandmothers. If your father or mother had stepmothers, include these women too.

Now, go back one generation. What do you know about the mothers of your grandmothers? Do you know anything?

From what you *do* know, what gifts and strengths are in you from your grandmothers? What vulnerabilities? How are you different?

From what you know, what gifts and strengths are in you from your great-grandmothers? What vulnerabilities? How are you different?

Finally, take some time to reflect on your own mother. What gifts and strengths in you are from her? What vulnerabilities? And how are you different?

Now, address the following prayers to these women:

> "I pray for your courage and strength, Grandmother; stand here beside me."

> "I pray for your vulnerability and feeling, Grandmother; stand here beside me."

> I pray for your care and your power, Grandmother; stand here before me."

> "I pray not to forget you, Grandmother; stand here beside me."

> "I pray (here place your own petitions)_____, Grandmother; stand here beside me."

Complete the practice by breathing quietly in thanksgiving for the lives of these women, and by mourning what has been forgotten about them.

The additional part of this practice may take some time. But if it is possible, engage in the work of discovering the women who are your past at least back to your grandmothers' grandmothers.

Practice 6: Imagining Yourself As Dis-Coverer

Read the practice first. Then engage in the three preliminary steps.

1. With your eyes closed, imagine yourself on the search to dis-cover your spirituality. What are you wearing? What age are you? Are you alone? Are you with others? What is the place like? Are you indoors or outdoors? Stay with this imagining.

2. Imagine yourself coming upon what you are certain will be a discovery of your spirituality. What do you do? Are you quick or slow? Do you shout or are you silent?

3. Gradually, you uncover what you have found. What is it? What is your response? How long do you take?

4. Describe your discovery as if you were noting it in a journal or diary. Do you leave it, or take it with you?

5. Now imagine yourself returning from the search. Are you different? If so, how? If not, why not?

6. What does this imagining make you want to do during the rest of the day?

Conclude with at least two minutes of silent breathing.

Practice 7: Praying Your Spirituality

Read the practice first. Then engage in the three preliminary steps.

In this chapter, Dis-Covering was added to Awakening. Our spirituality now includes both these steps. This practice draws on them and asks you, as in the last chapter, to pray your spirituality.

After closing your eyes, and breathing rhythmically, allow your spirituality, wherever it is, to emerge from within your own depths. Be quiet and attentive to it. Listen to it. Use your senses. Dwell on the four strengths. Incorporate your vulnerability, your emotion, your caring, your connectedness. Incorporate . . . Incorporate . . . Incorporate. Have a gentle but intense conversation with your spirituality. Give it all the time it needs. What does your spirituality contribute to your dis-covering? And are the discoveries you are making now mainly of what is within you, or are they also of what is outside you? Do you find your spirituality a coming together of the within and without?

Before opening your eyes, take a few moments to celebrate your spirituality.

3

Creating

A Pause for Centering

As we begin our entrance into the third step, sit back in your soul. To do that, sit back in your body. Breathe gently and easily. This is the step of Creating, where we attend to the work of shaping our spirituality and giving it an artistic form. Let your reflections on Creating emerge from your inner self. Take time, don't hurry, and try to spend at least a few moments with each question. Do the same thing with each of your responses.

Begin by returning in memory to your childhood. Recall an incident from your childhood when you did something creative—anything from putting on a play to solving a math problem to helping a neighbor with a quilt. Try to recall this creative moment in detail, spending a few minutes recapturing the feeling of that time.

Now think of your teenage years. Recall an incident when you were a bit older and again did something creative—anything from planning a school debate to planting vegetable seeds to writing a poem. How did you feel, knowing creativity was a part of you?

Reflect now on your adult years. What memories stir when you remember creativity during your adult life? Where is your creativity concentrated now? Is it mainly in one area of your life such as homemaking, work, child care, or sports? Or is it rinsed through everything you do?

Who are the most creative women you know? The first people you think of when asked to name someone creative?

What is it about them that makes you call them "creative"?

Are women more creative than men?

Are children more creative than grown-ups?

What about the woman you are, compared with the men you know? What about the child in you—is she still there in the woman?

If and when you imagine God, is God a Creator, or a Creative Spirit?

If so, what does God create? And how?

Might God be dwelling within you, ready to guide you through the step of Creating your spirituality?

At times in our lives when we feel relaxed, or "loose," we often find ourselves humming or singing or dancing. If we are feeling especially free, we even sense that we are not just singing a song, we are the song; we are not just listening to music, we are the music; we are not just doing steps in rhythm, we are the dance. We lose the distance and separateness that are often a part of our everyday lives. And instead we feel a connectedness and relation to the deep undercurrent that forms the rhythm of the universe itself—the same rhythm that is expressed in day following night, and spring following winter. We recognize that in some profound way we are part of that universal rhythm: We are creators, we are poets, we are the music and the dance.

Actually, this experience is not a new one in women's spirituality. Our twelfth-century foremother, Hildegard, taught that awareness of music heralded awareness of God. She prayed to the Divinity with the words, "You are music," and said that without our hearing music, our "understanding of the whole" could not happen. It is our way to wisdom, and certain other mysteries are learned through music that are learned no other way. Throughout Hildegard's teaching, music in all its forms announces the presence of God.

In the step of Creating, we incorporate this realization, adding to it the knowledge that we, too, are a kind of music,

> ". . . music heard so deeply
> That it is not heard at all, but you are the music
> While the music lasts. . . ."

We also begin to attend to the truth that the music we are is a symbol of our spirituality, and that within us lie capacities and abilities, *powers*, to create that spirituality and to *be* it. And the possibility of acknowledging and claiming all this comes when we pause and become serious about the vocation to be a Creator.

Now is the time to dance in the step of Creating. Having Awakened to our spirituality and Dis-Covered its main features, we take upon ourselves the vision of the creative artist. Attentive and alive to the deep inner music that is our life, we now take the "stuff" of that inner life and engage in the work of giving our spirituality a *form* of its own. During this part of our spirit's dance, we do that by taking the time to see (a) what creating means, (b) what its laws are, and (c) the steps in its process, in order to shape the spirituality that most becomes us.

What Creating Means

Although the word "creating" resonates with overtones of a Creator *Spirit*, or a Creator *God*—the first words of the Bible are "In the beginning God *created* heaven and earth"—the fact is that not only God, but all human beings engage in the activities of forming, shaping, and molding which are at the center of Creating. Artists and philosophers zero in on the meaning of creating by speaking of the artistic act as the creating of *form*; even more, as the creating of form which expresses human feeling and human being. They often speak of the act of Creating as molding and giving form to *life*, and for many people the most intense creative activity they engage in is forming and shaping their lives into works of art. Educators reflect more on the *qualities* that accompany the creating of form, such as *originality*, *uniqueness*, and *novelty*. And researchers on creativity tell us that certain *attitudes* will tend to develop as we engage in creating: *sensitivity*, or more accurately, *sense-ability*, where all of our senses become awake and alive to their surroundings; *flexibility*, the capacity to live regular2- with a range of possibilities, rather than being stuck with only one; and *fluidity*, the capacity to see many solutions to a problem. Yet everyone who talks about Creating agrees it is not foreign to any of us and just not true when a person says, "I'm not creative." For all human beings *are* creative to start with, and anyone can deepen and develop her creative power as she lives her daily life. It is this last aspect of creating that concerns us at this step.

The Creating in Every Day

As soon as we pause to examine our lives as women, we find that we are always engaged in some form of creating. We may not be painters or poets, but we often spend our days breaking through old visions into new ones; making suggestions to our children about ways they can overcome hurt at school; and imagining what an old recipe would taste like if we changed one of its ingredients. We delight in putting colors together in new combinations and in bringing people together in new relationships. Some of us even create organizations like Mothers Against Drunk Driving or Women's Action for Nuclear Disarmament. Like vulnerability, emotion, care, and connectedness, creating is no stranger to us.

Two Images of Creating

The imagery surrounding spiritual Creating, however, has taken two very different forms in religious history, and it is critical to be aware of them. The first is an image of Creating as the work of a builder, or a carpenter, where creators do their molding and shaping *outside* themselves. In this image we construct something; we "create" a product, whether it is a pie, a party, or a marketing plan. We can stand back from it, be separate and apart from it. We and the thing we made are distinct. In this imagery, creating is *making*, and the image is reflected in phrases like "making" meaning or "making" love or "making" a living. In this first image, making is something one can *work* at, and often ends up in the belief that we can make anything we want if only we try harder.

    The second image is quite different, and we saw evidence of it in the step of Dis-Covering, when with Julian of Norwich we found God enclosed in us, and ourselves enclosed in God. In this second image, creating is a brooding, caring activity carried on as if by "an eagle . . . that flutters over its young." (Deut. 32:11) It is a life-giving energy and intuition and inspiration that go on from *within*, where the person creating is never separated from what she is shaping, and where the closest analogy is birth. In this second imagery of the creative process, we are never cut off from the source of life, and nature itself, including human nature, "is never spent . . . because the Holy Ghost over the bent world broods, with warm breast and with ah! bright wings."

    In such an image, we breathe Creating in; we dwell in it and are shaped by it. We are raised up and carried by this inward power—which poet Gerard Manley Hopkins called the "inscape" of things—and the creating occurs in communion between ourselves and the source of life. Such creating is never finished or over; instead, it is a mirror of the universal creating we experience in the seasons, the tides, and the continuing rhythms of breath and blood, life and death, which create and re-create us all. This second imagery which guides us as we dance is especially evident in the poetry of the Hebrew Bible:

> You give breath, fresh life begins,
> you keep renewing the world. (Ps. 104:30)

> The Spirit of God has made me, and the Breath of the
> Almighty gives me life. (Job 33:4)

> As long as my breath is in me, and the spirit of God is in
> my nostrils. (Job 27:3)

The Laws of Creating

Four laws assist us as we begin. The *first* is framed in the Buddhist teaching:

> However hard you search for it
> You will never be able to grasp it.
> You can only become it.

Here is the law that refuses to separate creator and created, that teaches us that *we become what we create* and that, like birth, it is not possible to hurry the process. Rather than our thinking of ourselves as working toward a "goal" or "objective"—"What's the five-year plan for my life?"—this law instructs us to be wary of *effort* and *production* and to be more attentive to *allowing* and *permitting* the forces of life to shape us. Following such a law leads us *into* something if we let it and is far more attuned to living questions than living answers. In spirituality, this is the base of practices such as meditation, contemplation, Zen, and Sabbath, all of which tilt more to the side of not-doing rather than doing, and of not-knowing rather than knowing. This first law is also at the base of the creative quality of *sensitivity*, where we give our senses, especially our sight, time to know what they see, rather than limit them to seeing what they know. And, by teaching us the refusal of striving and grasping, this law permits us to cultivate the capability to live in uncertainty, doubt, and mystery without needing to know "why."

The *second law* is born from this one and teaches that *Creating is a continuing process.* This means in part that once we engage in the step of Creating, we take on an ongoing, never-ending movement. At no point *in our lives* will Creating be complete, because at no point will we know all that we can know, be all that we can be. (Despite the U.S. Army's advertising that we can!) At no point in our lives will all the data be in concerning who we are and what we are called to be. Instead, we will come to recognize Creating as a step in the dance of spirituality to which we return—as we do to each of the steps—many times in life, although if our spirituality is a living one, each time it will be at a deeper level.

This ongoing process, the Creating Process, will always include a rhythmic series of moves. We have undoubtedly already known and lived them, at least subconsciously, under other names, but I call them *Contemplation, Engagement, Formgiving, Emergence,* and *Release.* These are steps familiar to every artist, and they form the base for the next part of this chapter. But what needs emphasizing here is that these five steps are not like steps of a staircase or a ladder. Instead, just as with the entire dance of the spirit, these are understood best as steps in rhythmic movement, involving motion backward and forward, bending and bowing, periods of waiting, and a deep inner music.

The *third law* is true at each of the other steps, but needs to be highlighted here. This law says, "<u>You do not create alone.</u>" You *never* create alone. In the realm of spirituality, Someone or Something is always creating with you; Someone is always creating *you.* As at the step of Awakening, where Someone helped awaken us, and at the second step where Someone or Something was searching for us—as we were searching— so now, at the third step, we follow a law saying we do not have to do it all ourselves. The brooding, hovering presence we have already met holds us gently and tenderly in its everlasting arms, at times making us lie down in green pastures, at others leading us beside still waters.

And the *fourth law* is paradoxical. The only way to ensure Creating is to do away with preexisting ideas of what our spirituality will look like after we have moved through the process. Like all artistic work, presupposing the outcome can only get in the way. So we must put our assumptions aside and be willing to risk birth—as all genuine creating must. J. D. Salinger once captured the essence of this fourth law in telling the story of the little boy Buddy, listening intently as his ten-year-old brother Seymour, arguably the greatest marble player in all of Brooklyn, instructed him in that particular art. Seymour's counsel was this: "*Could you try not aiming so much?*"

The Steps in
the Creating Process

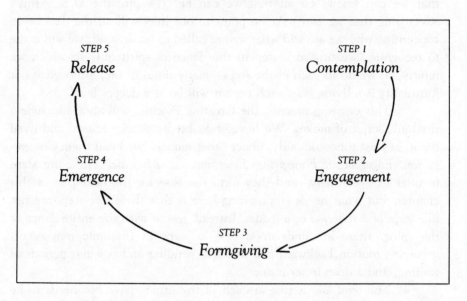

STEP 5
Release

STEP 1
Contemplation

STEP 4
Emergence

STEP 2
Engagement

STEP 3
Formgiving

Step 1: Contemplation

The first step in Creating is Contemplation. This is the moment where looking and seeing are our principal work. The creative process begins with our attempting to see what is there in our spirituality with our being still and quiet and not rushing in, just as we do when creating a meal, a home, a book, or a poem. We look *intensely* at spirituality, not so much at its individual features, but as a whole, something we have not yet done specifically until this Step. And by naming this step "contemplation," we draw on a religious, spiritual understanding, where what we look at is approached as a "*Thou,*" toward which we bring an attitude of reverence and respect. Religiously, contemplation means gazing at something with an uncluttered view, being as wide-awake as possible, and attempting to be as free from preoccupation and preconception as we can. Religiously, contemplation acknowledges we are in the presence of more than ourselves—it is a form of prayer.

Writer Annie Dillard, who is something of a modern mystic, tells a story of her own childhood which helps explain the meaning of contemplation. When she was a little girl, she used to be seized by the compulsion to hide pennies along the sidewalk, or in the branch of a tree, as a gift for someone else to find. Before she could write she drew arrows toward the pennies, and after she learned to write she labeled her arrows "Surprise ahead," or "Money this way." But, she tells us, she never lurked about waiting to see what happened. Instead, it was enough simply to think of the happiness of the passerby who found it, receiving in this way a free gift from the universe.

Now, as an adult, Dillard thinks back to this childhood joy and realizes it holds great meaning. For wherever we are, and wherever we go, there are "lots of things to see, unwrapped gifts and free surprises." For Dillard, the world is "studded and strewn with pennies cast broadside by a generous hand," but far too often we are too tired or too unseeing to notice. We miss what is there before our very eyes. Yet if we do cultivate an inner poverty, an inner serenity; if we cultivate the capacity to contemplate; if finding a penny can literally make our day, "Then, since the world is in fact planted in pennies, you have with your poverty bought a lifetime of days." And she concludes, "It is that simple. What you see is what you get."

"What you see is what you get." Not only does Annie Dillard teach the meaning of contemplation in that story, she also offers an understanding of spirituality. For initially, spirituality is seeing. This means not just looking but *seeing* what is actually there, seeing into and entering the deep places and centers of things. Spirituality means recognizing pennies everywhere, strewn broadside by a generous hand. Apples are pennies, cocker spaniels are pennies, rocks and rivers are pennies, even people are pennies. The Creating in our spirituality begins with our cultivating the inner eye that sees everything as capable of being—in my friend Dulcie's phrase—"saturated with God."

Barriers to such seeing existed for several centuries in what we now realize were false teachings about spirituality. These teachings said that if a person wanted to deepen her spiritual life, she would have to deny her body and go off to some spiritual realm, untouched by the messiness of material things. Here, *spiritu*ality, as the word in part suggests, had to do with people becoming like angels—pure spirits *without* bodies. In addition, if a person wanted to practice spirituality with any seriousness, she really should be a nun. And if that wasn't possible, she should at least try to live like a nun, which among other things, wasn't fair to the humanity of women who were nuns. From this point of view, spiritual life could be lived only by withdrawing from the world and living in a safe place, such as a convent, where you had to be *unselfish*, rather than learn to love yourself and center your thoughts and feelings on God as much as possible. You also had to avoid anything or anyone that would distract you from the pursuit of goodness: things like dancing, partying, or celebrating, as well as things like buying a new dress, enjoying a glass of wine, or using perfume. Not only was spirituality serious business, it was *solemn* business, and a good hearty laugh had no place in it.

And then there was God. In this way of seeing, God was a judge: a stern, unsmiling, powerful judge, waiting to pounce whenever we deviated in the slightest way from what "good girls" or "nice women" or "ladies" did or did not do. God was always compiling lists about us, and those lists most often had more things listed under *bad* than under *good*. If we made even one mistake we were out of favor with God forever, having to get ourselves back into God's good graces by spending months and years of making up for what were actually only human mistakes. And of course God was male—generally an older male—an old man with a white beard sitting on a cloud in the sky. God was white too, not Black, Asian, or Red Indian.

Any woman contemplating the meaning of spirituality is aware of these once-common understandings; their traces are still with us. Yet today, when we look at spirituality reverently, in the Step of Creating, we find that such views have fallen apart, and in their place a new, more genuine and more whole spirituality has been created.

This new spirituality begins with our taking womanhood seriously. We are refusing to accept definitions or meanings of what it is to be a woman from outside ourselves, whether these come from psychologists, physicians, or priests. We are deciding it is more important to be *whole* than to be *good*. Throughout the world we are telling one another our own stories, describing our lives as women, and learning to cherish our bodies. We are less fearful of human feeling than we have ever been, and we are more positive and delighted by the gift of sex. We are Dis-Covering, as we saw at the Second Step, that our powers are great ones, without which the world would lose much of its luster.

We have also stopped withdrawing. We have become aware of ourselves as being involved in the world, whether that involvement is through a job outside our home or within it, volunteering to help the homeless, or adopting a handicapped child. We have begun to take seriously our responsibility *to* other people, and *for* the part of the world that depends on us to speak for it: the animals, trees, air, and water. We have also begun to take seriously the belief that God is found in the midst of life, and that one of the places for meeting God is our own hearts.

And that signals what may be the greatest change of all. Contemplation is leading us to realize we must change our images of God and that to imagine God as judge, or distant figure removed from human life, is to do a disservice to God. We must recognize a God who continually broods over and warms us, yet is beyond all our imagining. We are beginning to realize that any God Who is God can be understood and appreciated as Mother as well as Father; as Black as well as Red; as Rice as well as Bread. Perhaps best of all, we are realizing that God always has and always will be on our side.

Contemplation such as this allows us to move toward Creating a richer understanding of spirituality than we have ever known. Acknowledging the new situation teaches us that at this time and at this place spirituality is at least this: *Our way of being in the world: surrounded, held, cherished, touched by, and bathed in the light of the Mystery of God.*

First it is *our* way, ours as women, who are neither children nor men. Second it is a *way*, which means it has a form, a shape, and a direction. Third, it is our way of being *in the world*, the only place we can live. And fourth, it is our way of being in the world *in the light of knowing we are held by the Divine Mystery* who loves us and who desires that we become ourselves, alert to and living out the full range of our possibilities. As the poet Anne Sexton has put it, we "cannot walk an inch without trying to walk to God."

Step 2: Engagement

Every artist knows you cannot keep *looking* at your materials; you cannot keep reading the recipe; you cannot remain at a distance. In this step, you must do more than merely *contemplate* spirituality. And so gradually, we dance from Contemplation into *Engagement*, where the movement is shaped by diving in, wrestling with, sinking into, and *meeting* our spirituality. Engagement is the step for plunging in and messing around. It is the step of taking spirituality on, committing ourselves to getting inside it, and allowing it to get inside of us.

I often introduce this second movement by asking women to take a ball of clay, the color of earth, and explore, search, and live inside the material in order to meet the form that inhabits it. "With your fingers and your hands," I tell them, "search for the shape hidden inside the clay. Close your eyes and allow your sense of touch to guide you." They must take on interplay and interchange with the clay—just as the clay will explore and search them in return.

The point is, Engagement is the beginning of a relationship, and as they work with the clay, it works with them, often giving them insight and a sudden change of direction they were not expecting. They follow the fourth law and learn to stop aiming. "I wanted the clay to look like a tree I was picturing in my mind," said one woman, "but it kept resisting and telling me to go another way. So I suddenly found myself talking to it, and asking, 'Is this what you want me to do? Is this what you want from me?' " The clay symbolizes our spirituality in this interaction, and it leads us to feel, with our hands, the experience of engaging with and living inside something.

Specific practices and exercises help here, much as they do when we decide to lose weight, or learn a new game, or speak a new language. Practices and exercises symbolize the commitment we make to engage with all that is. When we are willing to go where practices and exercises lead us, we find we are traveling a route toward Communion, and when we come to the Fifth Step, Nourishing, we will look at the meaning of practices and spiritual disciplines more closely. For now, however, I want to point out that the daily twenty minutes offered at the end of each chapter is designed as a time for connecting with the deeper engagements of our lives.

Because it *is* diving in and living inside, that time helps us connect with our deeper selves, our thoughts, dreams, and desires, and even with our unique *circumstances*, such as raising our children alone, working two jobs, or being too old to live by ourselves. Once we are engaged with our own depths, we can then move on to engagement with other selves. Our strengths of community and connectedness have the ability to deepen the consciousness of that life-giving well in *each* of us, met in Dis-Covering. We can begin to *live* from that engagement, treating others with the same reverence we are showing ourselves, and become sensitive to their fears and their griefs too. One college senior, describing this engagement, talked of her gratitude in finally emerging from a period when she was so caught up in her own "identity crisis" that she could not acknowledge the reality of other people. Now, however, she has lived into this part of the step.

And that living, if we do not curtail or abort it, can then lead to engagement with others, this time the nonhuman inhabitants of the planet Earth. Deeply spiritual people, often those close to the land who have not gone to school much, have always manifested such engagement. During the 1940s, Air Force officials were astonished at the ease with which Eskimos got damaged planes to work smoothly and put them back into service. When they examined the situation more closely, it became clear the Eskimos thought of the planes as alive. They saw circulatory systems and nervous systems in the planes. And so they approached their work with a kind of prayerful, even mystical attitude of offering "healing" to the planes. Another people who manifest this are Native Americans. They have never hurt or raped the earth the way white people have because they have seen the Great Spirit's presence in everything: the sun, moon, trees, wind, and mountains. They have also approached the Great Spirit *through* these things, as many of us non-Indian women are now starting to do.

Which brings us to a final form of *Engagement*, with the One Who is the Ground of all engagement—the One Who Creates: God. As we saw when we dis-covered divinity, this form of engagement is generally *not* with the Great Spirit directly, but with the Great Spirit as She is present in the midst of all our other Engagements. We do not come face-to-face with *the* Face as *separated from* so much as *in the midst of.* The Spirit, the Heart, the Mystery at the Center of everything is with and under and over and through all creation.

And when we are engaged with that Mystery, we learn what all genuinely spiritual people have known before us—Engagement is awe-full. Engagement pushes us down onto our knees, the way great moments of human birth and human death do. Engagement makes demands. Once we become truly involved in Creating, it is very difficult to withdraw, no matter how hard we try. We are impelled to do something and to be something that strikes us as incredibly complicated because it seems to be a not-doing and a not-being, similar to the waiting of pregnancy. If we want to allow the continuous, creative unfolding of the dance in which we find ourselves now, it will probably mean we must change our lives. Not, however, in the direction once thought of as the only way: "giving things up." Instead, it will be in the direction of "allowing things in." Engagement will demand we reshape and re-form our way of being in the world—our spirituality—in such a way that we throw out the barriers to Communion and become the mystics we have the potential to be.

Step 3: Formgiving

The step of Engagement may be relatively brief for some. Others will stay in it longer, savoring the facets of their spirit's life, dancing in slow time, and in no hurry to move on. But at some point in Creating, a new step, *Formgiving*, will claim us. As a result of the meeting and wrestling and acting-upon from our side, and the acting-back-upon from the other side, the process will reach the moment when *a new form begins to be created*. If we stop and look, we will see that Engagement has given way to a step where our spirituality is taking on a form and design of its own. We are now passing over into the security of *Formgiving*.

At this step, most of our energy will go into the continued molding, brooding, and hovering which are meant to shelter and encourage the new form. And depending on the communities that surround and support us, the personal histories we carry within us, and the circumstances influencing us at the time, these forms will vary, although there will be aspects of each form in everyone. For some of us, the dominant way of expressing our spirituality will be through our bodies, and we will give form to a *Physical* spirituality. We will be the ones who do not just dream of traveling, but who get up and go. We will not be content as audience; we will walk onstage and act. We will not just stop and smell the flowers; we will dig our hands into the earth as planters of gardens and tillers of soil. When people we know are sick, it will not be enough for us to give them a call, because talk alone does not suffice. Instead, we will have to bring them something we've made, or take in their laundry, or baby-sit their children. A physical form of spirituality will fit us best, because we are most ourselves before the Spirit of God when we are active and "in touch." We make the great contribution of reminding others that God is found at the physical center of life, and in its concrete detail, or not found at all.

Other women's way of being in the world will be as seekers and questers. These are the ones who will give form to a *Questioning* spirituality, molded by assuming there is always more than meets the eye; that there is always Mystery. This may be our form, especially if we are a person usually on the move and for whom putting down roots is rarely an option. It may also be our form if it is characteristic of us to "wonder" at things and people—not the wondering of gossip, but the wondering of awe. Or it may prove to be the form for us only at certain periods of our lives. I had dinner recently with a new friend, who has now lived in the United States for seven years. As we talked about her leaving her home in Germany, alone and for good, I said, "That must have taken great courage." Her answer was, "No, it was something I had to do. I had to follow the question of what life was like here. It is my way."

When and if this is our way, we can be comforted by the truth that the women who question and wonder—who are never satisfied with the status quo—are among those who have brought us today into the new and dazzling light of women's spirituality. For they have been the ones asking, "Isn't there more to life than this? Isn't there more to spirituality? Isn't there more to God?" Like one of the characters in Alice Walker's great novel, *The Color Purple*, they say, "I think us *here* to wonder."

Or, as we contemplate life and engage with it, we may give form to a *Resisting* spirituality. If we are people who possess heightened awareness of injustice, not only in our own lives, but in the fabric of the world, the main form we give to our spirituality may be resistance. Religious people have usually called this "prophecy," because prophets, especially in the Bible, are people who cry a great "No!" to injustice and evil. If we are people who from the time we were small have somehow noticed there are "haves" and "have-nots" and that someone has to resist, even rebel, against that situation, this may be our form.

But it may also be our form if we are regularly aware of the need to face evil and name it, the need to acknowledge that in our own sorry century as well as the centuries before us, the innocent have been slaughtered, the children have been massacred. It may be our form if we weep over history, where the hands of the human community have been bloodied in circumstances where bleeding was *not* a blessing—from the blood of the Innocents at the hand of Herod to the blood of at least one million children of the Holocaust.

Resisters are those who face the awful truth that injustice and evil come from within us, not from monsters who are not human and not from the animal kingdom, but from us, the human animals. ("With your clay, form something you *fear*," I say to a group of women. And they do, creating weapons and means of destruction—swords, knives, revolvers, bombs, nuclear missiles. They know the capacity for destroying is always there, inside.) But resisters also recognize the evil existing in social structures and political systems: in the backbreaking work of some so that others might be idle; in unequal, disparate pay and benefits withheld; in unfair legal practices that allow the guilty to go free. They recognize evil in apartheid or the neglect of the elderly or the rape of the land. For them, unless resistance to all of this exists in some form of spirituality, the ever-threatening power of evil remains unacknowledged.

Resisters live their spirituality by speaking for the bruised child, or sheltering the battered woman. Rather than give people a meal of fish—although they do that—they teach people *how* to fish. They are most themselves when working for better housing or better health care or better schooling for those who most need it. They are passionate about social issues, and in all honesty, some of us hate to see them coming because they so easily prick our consciences. They are people of whom their friends say, "She never seems to think of herself," or "She's a soft touch," when the truth of resisters' spirituality is that they are most themselves when confronting and changing the *circumstances* that damage lives. Such is their way of making the Mystery of God present to the world.

Or, as the creating process unfolds, a woman may realize she is giving form to an *Empowering* spirituality. If this is the characteristic shape our spirituality takes, we will be most at home when celebrating and fostering the growth of other people. We will be the ones who see gifts in others and work to have them use those gifts. Our own skills will go into encouraging others—often as teachers or mentors. We will be the ones who usually suggest that it is time to have a party to celebrate someone else's good fortune.

Empowering spirituality often blossoms for a woman when her children are small and her life is constant self-giving, but it may also be her characteristic way of being with everyone else. Empowerers tend to form their spirituality by making a home or a connection or an opportunity for someone else. Empowerers keep genuine love afloat in the world, especially if love means desiring good things for others. And although a woman may begin to give form to this way when she is a young mother raising children, she often discovers in her forties and fifties that she has grown into this way of being naturally. A friend reminded me of this recently. "My name is Gloria," she said, responding to a request she introduce herself to a large group, "and I think of myself as someone who helps other people find out who they are, and what contributions they can make in the world." The cup of her own spirituality is filled to the brim when the gifts within her overflow and touch others.

Finally there is a *Receptive* form of spirituality, present to a degree in everyone, yet at the center of some women's lives. Here is a spirituality of listening, of waiting, where we say to our souls, "Be still," or "Rest awhile," or—like the wise old woman—"Sometimes ah sets and thinks, but sometimes ah jes sets." Receptive spirituality has large moments of just "setting." It is a response to Pascal's comment that all the great troubles of the world come from the inability to sit still in a room by reminding us there are those who do precisely that.

For some women, receptivity is a natural mode. These are people who are instinctively reflective, who regularly take time to think things over before making judgments and commitments. Their natural wisdom is to sleep on things, and their lack of hurry often saves those around them from serious mistakes. They have never held the materialist view that "time is money" or that an idle mind is the devil's workshop. Idling, leisure, and stillness all have a contribution to make.

Other women live the same way; but receptivity has been given to them by life, just as much as they give it life themselves. They are bedridden, or palsied, or mentally unable. They are women who are ill or old, or in some way *forced* to be waiters and watchers, no longer able, if they ever were, to be completely involved in a physical, questioning, resisting, or empowering spirituality—although their receptivity may itself be a form of each of these. These are the women who experience life as something to be received in totality and are almost completely dependent on the care of others. They teach the rest of us much about a side of life that belongs in each of us but is too often ignored: a side of spirituality that sometimes arrives quickly, sometimes accidentally, yet eventually claims us if we live long enough. None of the other forms of spirituality is complete without its quiet dignity.

What may strike us most about these five forms, besides their not being an exhaustive list, is that they are not separable from one another, and that all of them are familiar. At the beginning of life we are full of *physical* energy, but we are also in some sense almost totally *receptive*— waiting for life to come and meet us. At the end of our lives we are forced to be *receptive,* especially as we befriend death, but this is often totally determined by our *physical* circumstances. And in the midst of, as well as in between both physical and receptive life, we all have periods of *questioning, resisting,* and *empowering.*

In fact, we discover as our spirituality takes shape that these forms are right for us in the face of certain events. Newly widowed, we may be forced to be totally receptive, permitting sorrow and loss into our lives, and allowing them time to do their healing work. If newly divorced, we may need to be totally resistant, refusing to be set back by feelings of failure. And if recently fired, we may need to be totally questioning, asking honestly where we were at fault, and assessing critically the conditions that made the firing happen. The beauty of these forms is that each is available to all of us whenever we need it, and should life demand from us the creation of a new form, the capacities to do so lie deep within us, in the music of our own creative dance.

Step 4: Emergence

Once we claim the form of our own spirituality, as well as allow it to claim us, we lean into the step of *Emergence*. Naturally following Formgiving, Emergence feels like a misty consciousness moving aside to reveal something forgotten. We stand at a new place, and yet it seems as if we are returning to a familiar one, but with a greater wholeness. Emergence provides a kind of substance and at-home-ness we did not have before. Our spirituality has been given form and we have formed it—at the same time. The recognition that this spirituality is *ours* and has personal *meaning* signals the move into Emergence. We now feel light, hope, joy; we feel set free.

For, having *Contemplated* the new meaning of spirituality for women of our time, and having been willing to do the difficult work of *Engagement*, we have moved through *Formgiving* to the place where our spirituality exists as a genuine creation. It has come forth, it has emerged, and from now on, even though we shall have periods of being rusty and out-of-touch, we can claim it and dwell within it. We have danced the steps of the Creating Process and come to the truth of ourselves as artists in the spiritual life. When this occurs, we must remind ourselves, as we did in the step of Awakening, that we are on holy ground, and once again must take off our shoes. We can *do* no more, except to take the last step in the creating process, the step of *Release*. Then we shall be the dance and the music. We shall be our spirituality.

Step 5: Release

All artists know the moment of release. In the shaping of clay, which we used as an example of the creating process earlier, a moment comes where we know it is time to leave alone what has been created—to stop working and let be. To let go as completely as we can. Release is that moment where we recognize in our bones that the first law of Creating is true: We no longer have a separate spirituality, we are one. Our spirituality has its characteristic form, of course, but it is not something outside ourselves. Instead, it flows through us like water in a sponge. It is us at our *most-self*.

In dancing the Seven Steps of spirituality, Release signals a moment that presses us to be completely still. When we do that, we find our attention captured not by our spirituality so much as by the Communion it carries, and by the Mystery at the center of the Communion. When this occurs, we need to release all conscious, intended moving in order to foster the letting go; the letting be. Allow the fourth step, *Dwelling*, to claim us. We are like Anne Sexton, who having engaged in what she called the "awful rowing toward God," found that finally the rowing ended. And so she moored her boat at the dock of an island called God and emptied herself on to the flesh of that Island.

We have come to a similar point. Although the creative process is a rhythmic and recurring one, the moment of Release signals the time to step away from Creating for a while in order to be *with* what we have become and to be *within* what we have formed. The moment of Release concludes, as did the step of dis-Covering, in letting go. But this time the letting go is not entrance into an active step like Creating. Instead, it is entrance into a step of tranquil rest—the step of *Dwelling*.

The Practice of Creating

Ideally, the seven practices of Creating are opportunities to engage in creating a fuller and more complete spirituality, as well as to cultivate an attitude of continuing creativity in your spiritual life. Ideally, you should practice at least one of them every day, giving yourself a full complement of fifteen or twenty minutes (which may be divided into parts and also expanded to twice daily, or forty minutes), even if you must rearrange your day. Done consistently, they will become rituals in your life, rituals that have their own rhythms and allow you to be creative and assist you in being so, as well as making Creating a permanent part of your spirituality. The preliminary steps for each practice are to:

• Sit comfortably and easily, in a quiet place if possible, but on a bus or a train if that is necessary.

• Shut out any outside noise by attentiveness to your inner self.

• Close your eyes and become attuned to your breathing, to the rhythm and pace of your breath. Be sure to spend—at this step—at least three minutes (180 seconds) coming to awareness of your breathing. Inhale gently; exhale gently. Feel your body as a place of rest. For some practices, you will need to open your eyes after these first three minutes; for others, the closing of your eyes is essential. You will discover for yourself for which ones it is necessary.

Practice 1: Your Senses as Companions in Creating

After closing your eyes, be aware of your eyes as they rest behind your eyelids. Feel them resting in their places. What will they see today? How will they assist you in meeting people today with an attitude of creativity? How will they assist you in looking at things—the created universe—with an attitude of creativity? Choose one person or thing you expect to be seeing today, and plan how you will take time to look at just this one person or thing as an element in creation.

After closing your eyes, be aware of your ears resting at the sides of your head. Feel them silently in their places. How can they help you today, as you listen, to be creative? Reflect on enlisting your ears to listen to yourself as you speak today, to listen to the words you will be speaking. Choose one creative word or phrase you will be using later in the day, and plan now to listen carefully to the ways in which you speak this word or phrase. Plan also to be attentive to hearing the creative words you will be hearing others speak.

After closing your eyes, be aware of your mouth, and of your tongue, your teeth, and the inside of your mouth. Feel them silently in their places. What taste will you incorporate into your life today to make your taste more creative? Even if it is something you eat or drink regularly, how might you eat or drink today so that it is in a new form, a form you have not used for eating or drinking regularly?

After closing your eyes, be aware of your nose, and of your nostrils, and the air coming in and being exhaled. Feel your nose as it gently breathes in and out. How might you use your nose, and your breathing, to find a new place today where you have never before been conscious of your breathing? Reflect upon, and choose now, a place you will be later today where you will stop, and be still, and breathe gently, with attention, for two minutes—a place you may then create as a place of breath.

After closing your eyes, be aware of your fingertips, and of the soles of your feet. Feel the surface your fingertips are touching; feel the shoes, or stockings, or surface touching your feet. What will your hands touch today that you might pick up, hold, and handle differently than you ordinarily do? What might you pick up, hold, handle, and then put together in a new form? A meal, an office, a shelf, a dress? Imagine yourself touching the things now, and plan to re-form them creatively during the day.

At the end of fifteen or twenty minutes, take another 60 or 180 seconds to be attentive to your breath. Then gently and slowly open your eyes, and conclude with either a spoken word or with a gesture to the Mystery within you as an act of thanksgiving.

You may find, after doing this practice, you want to concentrate on only one sense and not all five, or to concentrate on a different sense at a different time during the day. Go with your intuition, your instinct in all cases. You are the one to decide on the best way to spend these minutes. But try not to spend any *less* than fifteen or twenty minutes, to receive the full benefit of the practice.

Practice 2: Praying to the Creator Spirit

One of the oldest names for God is the Creator Spirit. The following is an ancient prayer to the Spirit, who can be thought of as He, She, It, or Thou.

Begin with the three preliminary steps. Then, *very slowly*, read the prayer, pausing at whatever line speaks to your inner self.

> Come Holy Spirit
> Send from your Dwelling-Place
> The brightness of your light.
>
> Come, Mother-Father of the poor,
> Come, Giver of Gifts,
> Come, Light of Hearts.
>
> Best of Comforters,
> Sweet Guest of the spirit,
> Sweet refreshment.
>
> Rest in labor,
> Cool respite in heat,
> Comfort in weeping.
>
> O most blessed light,
> Fill the inmost hearts
> Of your faithful ones.
>
> Without your Presence
> There is nothing in us,
> Nothing that is innocent.
>
> Wash the stained soul,
> Water the parched,
> Heal the wounded.
>
> Make supple the rigid,
> Warm the cold,
> Straighten the crooked.
>
> Give to your faithful
> Who trust in you
> Your sevenfold gift. *

*Traditionally, the seven gifts of the Spirit are Wisdom, Understanding, Counsel, Strength, Knowledge, Reverence (or Piety), and Awe

Give reward to goodness.
Give wholeness at the end.
Give joy everlasting.

Amen. Alleluia.

Practice 3: Contemplating Spirituality

Read the practice first. Then engage in the three preliminary steps.

This practice is an attempt to breathe, to contemplate your spirituality—your way of being in the world.

Choose one of the key words in the meanings of spirituality—"Communion," "Mystery," "Earth," "Spirituality"—or a word of your own choosing which "says" your spirituality to you.

Repeat this word in the form of a mantra. "Communion . . ." or "Mystery . . ." or "Body . . ." or "_____." Breathe in, inhale on the word, and then exhale.

Breathe in, hold, and exhale the word, gently, in a continuing rhythm, for example:

1—2—3—4 inhale the word;

1—2—3—4 exhale the word.

Continue to center upon the word for at least ten minutes. When your spirit signals to you that the time of contemplation is ending, stop the repetition of the word and breathe simply—simply breathe—with your eyes closed for at least two minutes.

Then open your eyes to conclude the exercise.

Practice 4: Creating the Opportunity to Find Pennies

Read the practice first. Then engage in the three preliminary steps.

This exercise is one where you must hold in your hand at least three, four, or five pennies. Spend at least five minutes on each part of the practice.

1. Hold the pennies in your hand and look at each one very carefully. Find out everything you can about each penny: its look, its date, whether it is shiny or dull.

2. Imagine each penny is a part of yourself, with your seeing it as a gift. Take time to let each penny tell you something about yourself you had not taken time to notice before.

3. Now imagine each penny represents someone you will see today, from the letter carrier, to your mother, to your best friend, to one of your children, to your boss. Ask each penny, now, to tell you or to remind you of something positive about that person.

4. After the exercise is over, "plant" each penny somewhere surprising—a place that will remind you of yourself, other people, the possibility of surprise. Think now of what those places will be (e.g. the freezer, the car, the medicine cabinet, your makeup case, etc.). When you come upon them during the day, take a moment to remember what the penny taught you.

Complete the practice by sitting silently with the pennies for at least two minutes. Then go and plant.

Practice 5: Molding Your Spirituality

Read the practice first. Then engage in the three preliminary steps.

For this practice you will need clay—purchased from an art store, or a five-and-ten—or some other soft material (even earth mixed with water will do) to serve you as you allow your hands to engage in molding.

After step three, when your breathing has become peaceful, do the following:

1. Take the lump of clay in your hands, and feel it, play with it, take time to get to know it.

2. Shape the clay into a ball or a sphere.

3. With your eyes *closed* (or if you think it would be a help, with a blindfold around your eyes), slowly and quietly form the clay into an image of your spirituality. Try not to prejudge what it will look like; do not even expect to make it into a recognizable shape, but let the form *emerge* through your working with it, and its working with you.

Give yourself at least five or ten minutes of this silent work.

4. Open your eyes and continue molding.

5. When you feel the form is complete, sit with it for a few moments. Allow it to speak to you and to tell you about itself, and about yourself.

6. Conclude with two minutes of silent breathing.

Practice 6: Plants and the Creative Life

Read the practice first. Then engage in the three preliminary steps.

Most women have at least one plant; many have several. The practice for this day is to choose one of your plants and to see what you might learn from it about your spirituality.

1. Begin by choosing the plant and sitting with it quietly.

2. Take a few moments, as long as you need, to contemplate the plant. Look at it, really look at it—its age, the size and color of its leaves, the stems, the places that seem to be budding, the places that seem to be dying.

3 Now, in your imagination, allow the plant to speak to you and to tell you about its life in your home or apartment. Allow it to tell you about a typical day. Take the time to be as genuine a *listener* as you can.

4. After listening, ask the plant what it can tell you about yourself and your spirituality. Again, in your imagination, take time to contemplate what about the plant is like you, what is unlike you.

5. Conclude the conversation and come to the end of the practice as you began, by sitting silently with the plant and allowing it to sit silently with you.

Practice 7: Dancing Our Spirituality

Read the practice first. Then engage in the three preliminary steps.

In this practice, we are asked to dance our spirituality. Dance is a common practice in women's spirituality—from the Shaker hymn, " 'Tis a gift to be Simple," where one shakes her sins away, to Tai Chi, the form of moving meditation danced by millions of Chinese today. The following is a dance that can be done alone or with others, to words or without them. Since many women dance secretly when alone, this may be one of our secret dances. But it can also serve as an image for other dances we ourselves create, which free us to be women of the spirit.

Words:	Gestures:
"Spirit of all living things"	Stand with palms facing your face. Slowly raise your palms high above your head.
"Create a new heart in me."	Slowly lower your palms, brushing your body with them and slightly bending, until your palms come to rest on your thighs.
"Spirit of all living things"	Stand with palms facing your face. Slowly raise your palms high above your head.
"Create a new heart in me."	Slowly lower your palms, brushing your body with them and slightly bending, until your palms come to rest on your thighs.
Verse 1:	
"Awaken me . . ."	Extend your hands forward . . .
"Dis-cover me . . ."	Embrace yourself lovingly . . .
"And lead me into Dwelling,"	Bow as deeply as you can.
"Spirit of all living things"	Stand with palms facing your face. Slowly raise your palms high above your head.
"Create a new heart in me."	Slowly lower your palms, brushing your body with them and slightly bending, until your palms come to rest on your thighs.
Verse 2:	
"Nourish me . . ."	Extend your hands forward . . .
"Tradition me . . ."	Embrace yourself reverently . . .
"And lead me to Transforming."	Bow as deeply as you can.

Repeat as often as desired. Do the dance in silence, to background music of your own choosing, or to the following melody:

Words and Music by Maria Harris

4

Dwelling

A Pause for Centering

Let us begin by being still. Sit back in your spirit; do that by sitting back in your body. This Fourth Step is Dwelling. Allow your personal reflections on Dwelling to emerge from your inner self. Breathe gently and easily. Let your breath find its own rhythm. Take time, don't hurry, and try to spend at least a few moments with each question and with each response.

In what place are you most yourself?

What are some of the characteristics of that place?

What are your feelings about the place?

Are there some places where you are more likely to feel at ease or at rest than others? If so, again, what are some of the characteristics of those places? Are they similar in some way? Or do they differ?

Are there some places where you are less likely to feel at ease or at rest than others? If so, again, what are some of the characteristics of those places? Are they similar to each other? Or do they differ?

Have you ever been in a place where you began to sense new things about yourself? A place that taught you about yourself, just by the kind of place it was? If so, what did you learn?

Are you most at ease and at rest when you are alone?

Are you most at ease and at rest with other people?

Or does the presence or absence of people at times and places of rest differ for you?

Do you sometimes want to be alone, at other times want company?

Do you visit imaginary places in fantasy or daydreaming? Do you spend much time in them? If you do, what calls you to visit them?

Did you ever visit imaginary places when you were a little girl? If so, have they remained a part of your life, a part of your memory?

Have you ever been homeless, without any dwelling at all?

Dwelling.

The sound of the word attracts. The meaning of the word comforts.

Dwelling.

To pause, to rest, to linger.

To abide. To stay for a while. To inhabit.

Dwelling.

To let things remain as they are for a time, to let be, to let go. To stop, and to let ourselves be surrounded by the joys—the healing joys—of rest, of contentment, of doing nothing.

Dwelling.

To give ourselves permission simply to *be*.

The Step of Dwelling has always been central in the spiritual life. Ordinary people as well as great mystics have known it was essential to go apart and rest awhile if their lives were to be complete. And so it is with us. Having Awakened to our spirituality, Dis-Covered its features, and undertaken Creating its form in our lives, we now reach the centerpoint of that spirituality: the place and time of Dwelling.

Awakening, Dis-Covering, and Creating all lead to Dwelling; while Nourishing, Traditioning, and Transforming all flow from it. Or, put in a slightly different way, the first three steps have an impulse *toward* this step; the last three steps have an impulse *from* it. But Dwelling is the step we find at the heart of Spirituality. Dwelling holds our spirituality together, knitting it into a seamless garment. In Dwelling we weave the fabric of our souls.

We begin this chapter by looking at the face and features of Dwelling and asking the question: "Dwelling—what does it mean?"

Then we ask a second question, *"Where* do we dwell?" and discover some very real places: places of sorrow, places of joy, places of work, and places of community. We discover too some ancient yet new ways to name those places: *Desert, Garden, City,* and *Home.* We take the time we need to examine each of these as a Dwelling Place for our spirits: a symbolic, centering, and spiritual location where we can live out the events and occasions that make up our inner lives. Finally, we move to the question, "With whom do we dwell?"

The Face and Features
of Dwelling

Place

Primarily, all Dwelling has to do with place. As human beings who are matter and spirit, body and soul, we must dwell some*where.* We may share that place—a house or apartment or room—with others, perhaps several others, parents and children and spouse. We may have the great luxury of a room of our own. Some of us may have both. But these are places of residence. We also dwell in places of work: an office, hospital, schoolroom, store. We dwell in places of daily travel: a car, train, bus, plane; a roadway, path, sidewalk. We dwell in places of worship: a church, temple, synagogue, chapel. We dwell in the open air, sitting perhaps by the side of a river. We dwell in places of recreation: a dance floor, exercise class, movie house. We dwell in restaurants. We dwell in art galleries. We dwell locally and intimately and individually in places personal to us alone—hideouts in the trees, and caves in the hillsides—and we dwell universally and majestically upon the ground of the planet we call Earth.

Each of these places affects the way we dwell. Some places are spacious and pleasing to the senses; others are cramped or cluttered, or decorated in a taste different from our own. Some are dark, dingy, dreary; others are flooded with light. I think of myself at the moment: I've just moved to a new apartment, smaller than the one I left. It is crowded with unopened boxes. I am continually looking for something or discovering I have misplaced something else.

Still, I've known other places that were perfect. Just right. Welcoming, as this place will be soon. Once I lived in Australia for six weeks and shared a flat. It was a perfect dwelling place, perhaps because my flatmate was an artist who knew the spiritual impact of environment. I realize I am deeply affected by a place, as all of us are. A place either cramps or expands us humanly.

The point of elaborating on the physical places in which we dwell at each moment of our lives is that for the step of Dwelling, we must seek out, for at least a few moments a day, a place where we can stop, be still, and linger. And if we cannot find an actual place, we need to create one in our imaginations. The pause for reflection at the beginning of each chapter and the practices at the end are best done if we are in a place where we *can* reflect. They are designed to make *Dwelling* a permanent feature in the geography of our spirits. They are designed to teach us that we need to create a regular place where we can go apart and rest a while every day.

At a level deeper than physical place, we dwell in spiritual places. Physical place can also be a symbol for those places where we exist and dwell spiritually: the mansions and rooms and gardens and theaters of our souls. Our spirits as well as our bodies can be cramped, crowded, cold, hungry, and ill at ease. Our spirits as well as our bodies can *also* be relaxed, enfolded, warmed, and comforted. Just as we can create physical places that ensure rich human dwelling, we can also create places within our spirits. If we attend to them with care, they can become places to carry with us always so that even if our physical dwelling changes, our interior place will always exist.

In the Step of Dwelling, we take the time to go into such places. We shut out distractions as much as we can and draw breath; we become quiet, and we say something along the order of: "Now I shall enter my secret place." That place is our soulroom, or spiritroom, and we are not being selfish when we take time to enter it. In fact, our moving to this room can make us more loving with other people when we emerge. A woman I know of, who teaches spirituality to little children, tells them the name of this special place is their "heartroom." So it is with us.

We have been attempting to do some of this dwelling at the beginning and end of each chapter—either in our pauses for centering or in our practices. I believe I can *promise* that once we begin to do these or similar interior exercises with any regularity, we will find that our exterior physical surroundings begin to differ. Just as they affect us, we will find that we affect them. The serenity and calm we develop through Dwelling will begin to flow to our outside environment. The physical places of our dwelling will begin to change because the Dwelling Place each of us *is* has begun to change.

And then we will start to witness a quiet miracle, as attending to interior dwelling influences exterior dwelling. Most of us can probably think easily of someone we know whose "place" is like that person herself: comfortable and serene. Now we are becoming this kind of person too. However, for this to happen, attention to *place* is not enough. We need attention to *time* as well. And so we come to the second feature of Dwelling, Presence.

Presence

For Dwelling to happen in us, we need not only to be in some *place*, we need to *be*—to exist and to live in some *time*. We need to be present. And being humanly present is often very difficult. We are always being tugged backward toward the past, or forward toward the future, and we are also always being tugged by the demands of those around us, often causing us to wish we were somewhere else. Sometimes that even pushes us into a make-believe existence where we fail to enjoy the present moment because we are thinking of a period that is over or a dreamtime yet to come. That is of course necessary for all of us occasionally, but when we spend too much time in a fantasy world, we *miss* much of our lives.

When we stop to think of it, we can be caught unprepared by how often we are not actually present! We are shocked by how often we have cheated ourselves of being fully alive! And that works two ways. Either we find ourselves with another person who is not present to us, or we realize in the midst of a conversation that *we* have not been listening. We say, or hear someone say to us in a frustrated tone, "You're not listening to me," or maybe, "You're somewhere else." The importance of this realization is critical, for if Dwelling is to occur, we must learn to cultivate Presence, care for it, and cherish it. The Mystery residing at the center of all that is does not reveal Itself to us unless we are willing to wait, to watch, and to *Dwell.*

Thich Nhat Hanh, who is a Vietnamese Buddhist monk, offers counsel in practicing presence by suggesting we attempt to be present in every activity of our lives: His example is washing the dishes. He says that if you are washing the dishes, the one thing you should be doing is washing the dishes, that is, be completely aware of the fact that you are washing dishes. He admits that at first that might seem a little silly because it seems like stressing a very simple thing. But he goes on to say that that is the point: The fact that you or I are standing here with cups and plates is a wonderful reality. It is an opportunity, as is every act, to be completely ourselves and to be conscious of our *presence*. The beauty of such moments is that if we stay present with whatever we are doing, there is then no way we will be tossed about mindlessly. Such a practice is particularly helpful when we are so busy we can't set aside a special time or place for Dwelling, because it enables us to encounter every moment as a time to participate completely in life. Such a practice comforts too, for although we cannot always go apart, cultivating presence ensures we *can* always rest awhile.

Most other religious traditions have similar practices. In Christian spirituality, the term "recollection" is sometimes used. "Recollection" is the practice of stopping and remembering where one is many times during the day in order to practice Presence, including remembering the presence of the Sacred in our Midst. That is the reason so many people use mantras—short, prayerful sayings like "Yes," or "Now," which tend to anchor the spirit. Personally, I have discovered that if I plan ahead during my morning moments of Dwelling to practice presence whenever I repeat a common daily activity—picking up the phone to make a call, signing my name—these actions become "cues" later on, reminding me to be present—to be where I in fact am. "While picking up the phone, be completely aware, Maria, that you are picking up the phone; while signing your name, be still, be quiet—dwell—and be completely aware you are signing your name." I can also attest that whenever I or anyone engages in such practices as these with care and regularity, we discover the third feature in Dwelling. A kind of stillness and serenity begins to permeate much of our lives, and even in the midst of action, we are at rest.

Rest

Rest, like Dwelling, is a humanly attractive aspect of life. It calls up images of tranquility and serenity. For busy, active twentieth-century women, rest has a particular charm, as we try to balance work, family, leisure, shopping, child care, traveling, and innumerable other aspects of our lives. Although too often we feel guilty when we wish for rest, we need to know the desire for it is embedded deep in the human psyche. We also need to know that the practice of rest, spiritual rest, is among the most ancient recorded practices of spirituality known to human beings. Rather than being a luxury, rest is a *law:* a law named Sabbath.

In the Hebrew Bible, Sabbath is taken so seriously that if you violate the Law of Sabbath, it is equal to breaking all of the law. Sabbath was, and remains for many Jews and Christians, fundamental to being a holy people. Second only to commands relating to the Creator, Sabbath tells people about themselves: Not only are we the creatures who honor parents, who do not lie or steal or murder, we are the creatures who, in the Image of the Creator, are called to do what the Creator did—to rest, and be still.

The form in which the Commandment was initially phrased is intriguing. It is, as *shavat*, a command to *not* do, to cease, to desist, to stop. Sabbath means, as the ancient Babylonian people phrased it, turning away from common activity in order to "quiet the heart."

The command extended to all human beings, women as well as men, and eventually became directed to the animals and the land. Animals could not be overworked or overdriven or mistreated. And the land was not to be bruised either. The land needed time, just as the animals did, to revive itself and be renewed. In other words, Sabbath was a distant early warning to human beings that all things are here on earth as gifts. Every element in creation is our companion and we may not manipulatively *use* one another. Treating creation as existing for us and us alone leads to its destruction, and our own too, as today's ecologists are teaching us. And so it is worth remembering this beautiful law, as it is found in the Bible:

> Remember the sabbath day, to keep it holy. Six days you shall labor, and do all your work; but the seventh day is a sabbath to the Lord your God; in it you shall not do any work, you, or your son, or your daughter, your manservant or your maidservant, or your cattle, or the sojourner who is within your gates; for in six days the Lord made heaven and earth, the sea and all that is in them, and rested the seventh day; therefore the Lord blessed the sabbath day and hallowed it. (Ex. 20:8–11)

Unfortunately, religious institutions and religious officials have often so overcontrolled the Sabbath with *man*-made rules and regulations, in contrast to the *divine* law, that the essential note is forgotten: It is *a commandment to rest.* The Sabbath is a commandment that tells us not only what to do, it is *a commandment that tells us what to be.* We are the beings in creation who rest. We are the beings who have a divine law within us—a law that says to us, "Periodically, you must rest. *You must dwell.* You must turn from the creating of the world to its Creator."

Many of us have so forgotten this spiritual meaning of rest that we have to be taught how to do it. My students often asked me, when I began giving instruction in Sabbath, "But, Maria, how do you *do* it? What are the rules?" And I would have to answer, "It is a not-doing. Rest means doing nothing, doing no thing. It means being receptive: to yourself and to others, to sorrow as well as joy. It means cultivating the ability to sit still in a room." Once again, "sometimes ah sets and thinks," says the wise old woman, "and sometimes ah jes sets."

I would also have to remind them, as I had to remind myself, that Sabbath is not only the seventh day of the week. Sabbath can be a period for as long as fifty days, as it is in the Sabbath of Pentecost, or even for as long as two years, as it is for the forty-ninth and fiftieth years called *Jubilee*—a clue to those in middle age. But it can also be a very brief time, suggesting to us that we might take many small Sabbaths in the course of a day. Rest, the characteristic feature of the Step of Dwelling, reminds us to bring a sabbatical attitude to all we are and do.

Where Do We Dwell?

If we stay with the Bible as a source just a bit longer, we are offered further keys to Dwelling. For the Bible is the story of a people which begins in a *Garden*, ends in a *City*, and throughout gives accounts of human beings wandering through the *Desert* in search of *Home*. This is true not only in the Hebrew Bible, but in the Christian Scriptures as well. And the key this gives us at the station of Dwelling is that we too live in Desert, Garden, City, and Home during the course of our lives. Not only are these real places—they are also symbols that name the Dwelling Places of our inner lives. Each place can be a set of circumstances out of which our spirituality deepens and emerges.

And though there are obvious overlappings in these dwelling places, the Desert reminds us that sometimes we dwell, whether or not we like it, in sorrow, emptiness, and endings.

The Garden reminds us we dwell in times and seasons of life-giving joy: from youth to maturity, from planting time to harvest, in the company of others as well as the Source.

The City reminds us we dwell in a world, in a culture, and in a society in which our human work can make a difference for the better.

And Home reminds us we dwell in dailiness, in care, in human love, and in community.

As we take the time to linger at each of these symbolic Dwelling places, we will probably discover we know each of them quite well. For we have already spent some time in all of them. We also may discover we need to spend more time in one or another of them if our spirituality is to be complete.

The Desert

Being deserted (or "desert-ed") and knowing the pain of loss is one of the universal human experiences. Whether it is being "dumped" by girlfriend or boyfriend, or later in life by a spouse or children, we all experience that pit-in-the-stomach agony that causes us to feel completely alone. But because of the extraordinary stress on pleasure in today's world, and because of the great emphasis on *having* rather than *being,* the importance and meaning of such "deserts" for today's women have tended to be diluted. We try to avoid pain, loss, and defeat rather than face them or, even more radically, befriend them.

Nevertheless, because suffering and sorrow are common to all lives, we must learn how to dwell in them. Certainly, I am not talking here about making suffering an idol, or anyone of us being a martyr or a victim: As women we have done this far too often. Nor am I talking about passively accepting the cruelty of others and allowing ourselves to be beaten or abused, even to the point of thinking we deserve it. Instead, I am talking about the inestimable value to our spiritual lives of learning to ride with the times when pain or sorrow strikes us.

Consider, for example, the experience of the end of a relation— one that has been a genuine relation of love. We feel loss; we wait for calls that never come; we are unable to eat. One temptation is to ignore the situation and to pretend we are not heartbroken inside. The opposite temptation is to wallow in our pain and to bring misery upon ourselves and all around us. Desert as Dwelling Place is neither of these. Instead, it is, as all dwellings are, a place and a time to face what is *here*—a time to be still and be at rest. Instead of for extra movement, it is an opportunity for extra quiet. It is a time for allowing ourselves to *feel,* to let the hurt wash over us, like great, healing waters, so that the desert inside can be faced and accepted. It is a time to acknowledge the wisdom of T. S. Eliot's words concerning times when we must be still; times when we tell our spirits to wait without any hope at all, because the hope would be hope for the wrong thing. These may even be times when we wait without love, and without seeking love, because that too might be love for the wrong thing. These even may be times when we know we must wait without feeling God's presence.

Another time we feel "desert-ed" is when we have reached a turning point in our lives and literally do not know where to go. No avenue is open to us; no hand is outstretched toward us; no other human being seems to be aware of us. Inside we are completely lost and empty. We are alone. One possibility is to rely on clichés—and sometimes this works—such as, "It is better to light one candle than to curse the darkness." But the desert as dwelling place can also be a positive setting where we take the time to dwell in darkness. We name it, face it, and come to grips with it. And out of our deep and quiet center, challenge it too. Instead of saying to our souls, "Be still," this time our mantra is "Rage, rage against the dying of the light."

When we find we have the courage to do this—and when we take this risk and survive it—we learn a great spiritual truth. We learn it is possible to go through hell and survive. We learn we have spiritual resources we did not know we had until this present moment. We come in touch with our own power, and a Power both within and beyond us—a Power we might want to name as God. And the desert as dwelling place loses some of its capacity to frighten us as we discover that although our *feeling* is the one described in the old spiritual, "Sometimes I feel like a motherless child," we are *not* children. Instead, dwelling in the desert teaches us we are strong, independent adult women.

The Garden

If the Desert is about dyings and endings, the Garden is about beginnings and flourishings, although it can teach us about certain endings too. The Garden teaches us about the rhythms of living upon the earth—with all the natural gifts that accompany those rhythms: food, shelter, shade; rest in labor, cool respite in heat, comfort in weeping. The Garden teaches of seasons and of decay. The Garden teaches us about being soil and being life givers. As soil and life giver, the earth is much like us and we are like it—we sustain each other. And this is especially true in the sustaining of our spiritual lives. One woman told me, after we had spent time together investigating spirituality, "I have discovered that there are practices going on in my life already that are spiritual but I had not acknowledged them as such. For example, my flower garden is a real source of joy . . . it is an escape for me from the tiresome into the Mystery, into the reality."

Perhaps even more than Sustainer, however, the Garden as Mother Earth and as Sister Soil is a metaphor for us as female beings-in-the-world. It tells us about ourselves and about our identity as women. "Earth you were once, unto earth you will return," goes the Ash Wednesday refrain. But rather than being sorrowful, such bonding with the earth provides profound and joyful insight. For it teaches us that every day of our lives we too *are* gardens—and gardeners as well: beginning again the digging and planting and tending of our own and other lives, and in doing so shaping and creating our worlds. Indeed a great part of the nurturing coming to us from the Garden is its teaching about our own ways of being and dwelling with the earth.

For the Garden is sometimes, as we are, a place of beginnings and a place of readiness—for pruning, for removal of weeds, and for receptivity to seeds. At other times, it is, as we often are as women, a dwelling place for exhaustion. Poet Marge Piercy reminds us of the connection. Just as the earth grows exhausted with being used and planted too much—remember Sabbath—so women are often seen as being worn out, as being too old. She even recalls to us our use of the term "dirt" as negative, as if we were not all children of earth, born ourselves out of that very same dirt, "the common living dirt."

At still other times, the Garden is, as we are, comfortable but not strikingly attractive, a dwelling place for growing old. At some point in our lives—somewhere in our forties or fifties or sixties—we come to terms with the truth that, like the earth, we are aging, becoming "frayed and nibbled survivors," who are, in Annie Dillard's words, "getting along." No longer are we particularly beautiful or even pretty. Yet we are capable of bearing fruit, and as the seasons pass and blend into one another, we find that the years let us bear a certain kind of riper and fuller fruit, not possible when we were young. These fruits are the wisdoms and insights and secrets we have culled from living through several decades, and they give us a strength, a stability, and a joy that cannot be forgotten.

For what the Garden as Dwelling Place offers us is knowledge of possibilities and seasons in which we dwell throughout a lifetime—from girlhood to maturity. It gives us the soft and early light of spring accompanied by the strength and violence of thaw and flooding and roots breaking through rock, our being born anew from a kind of androgynous childhood into the power of sexuality. It gives us the long hot summers, where we learn to wait for the rains. And it gives us the wisdom of autumn light, which catches us up short with how brief life is, and how precious and priceless is the gift of even "one autumn crocus, one lavender aster, one brilliant orange maple."

Perhaps most of all, however, the Garden teaches us mutuality. Although the earth gives us sustenance and identity, the flowering and fruitfulness of the Garden do not happen unless we tend it and work with it. We are not passive recipients to what it brings. Instead, we are tenders and tillers of the soil, both the soil of the earth and the soil of our own souls. The breadth and length and depth of our spirituality is, in part, up to us.

When we do take responsibility for the Garden of our spirit, we gradually make the discovery that as we have been tending, so too has Another. We have been part of a mutual engagement, a mutual relation. One woman told me this about herself:

> The new life that is the result of this [spirituality] process is vulnerable, demanding, fragile, hungry, out-crying, dependent on other nurture for continued existence . . . I once thought spirituality to be a privatized thing. It was what I "did" internally in an attempt to find God. Instead, all along, it was God who was seeking me, and I was refusing to come out, opting to stay in the gestating place, in the dark . . . My spirituality has been born, and now I will seek to remain aware of my dependence on other sources for continued life, seek to allow the growth to happen, not to hinder it, *seek and receive* the nurture that is there for me, given through others by the Source of Life.

The City

If Desert and Garden were our only Dwelling Places, we might succumb to the danger of forgetting that we dwell in a cosmos and a world with innumerable other creatures—both human and nonhuman. The glory of the City as Dwelling Place, either as an actual city or as a *symbolic* reaching out to others on a local, national, or *global* level, is its capacity to center us in relation. One of the great Dis-Coveries we made about our spirituality as women in chapter 2 was its emphasis on assisting others to develop, and on connectedness. In the city as Dwelling Place we live this out.

When we dwell in the City, our mantra is the ancient spiritual maxim: "*Contemplata aliis tradere*": *Contemplata*—the fruits of spirituality and of contemplation: *aliis*—to others; *tradere*—are to be handed over, given away. Simply put, "The fruits of our spirituality are to be given away to others." To hoard spirituality and spiritual gifts for ourselves will make us spiritually sick, because as human beings we have a *capacity for the universe*. To remain in our secret place without eventually leaving it is unhealthy. To not care about society is to violate the law of our being: We must love one another or die. Just as *not resting* is the violation of a law, so is *not loving*. The City is the symbol not only for our dwelling in that conviction—it is the Dwelling Place where we do something about it.

Women operate from this Dwelling Place in many different ways. Through the centuries, it has been for some the center of their spiritual lives. For example, women such as the Beguines of the Middle Ages, who were neither nuns nor married women, banded together to be of help to others. There are women in health care who have given themselves to nursing the sick and the dying; religious groups of women whose purpose for coming together in community was and is to feed the hungry, give drink to the thirsty, shelter the homeless, visit the imprisoned, and assist those who are abused and battered. Other women whose work is outside their homes—police officers, social workers, and secretaries—do not act in such a direct fashion, yet they bring to what they do the same, or similar caring attitudes. And in still other cases, caring work forms the bulk of the days of women who work at home. These are women who officially or unofficially earn the titles Daughter of Charity and Sister of Mercy.

Other women enter the City for a few hours a week or only periodically, doing volunteer work in nursing homes (one told me recently that her own mother had received such tender care before her death that she wanted to care similarly for other aged women), in hospitals and hospices, in day care centers, in schools and other service organizations, feeling their spirituality is incomplete unless they do. Still others operate soup kitchens, help with breadlines, give time in "houses of hospitality," as the *Catholic Worker* refers to its shelters, or alert others to places homeless women can go and be taken in. Some women care for the nonhuman animals through animal shelters, antivivisection movements, and organizations to save various species, such as those to save the whales. Still others live in the City as Dwelling Place by being friends of the Earth and working to end pollution and the rape of the environment. Or, like the women at Greenham Common in England, to end the threat and possibility of nuclear disaster.

Wherever a woman works to answer a need, the City is her Dwelling Place. An hour ago I spoke on the phone with a woman whose work is called Bread of Life—the bread going to the hungry in Haiti. A week ago, I spoke with a woman who is a chaplain in a correctional facility for women, whose work throughout the year includes finding homes near the prison where the children of prisoners can live and visit their mothers daily. A day ago, I met a woman who brings meals to AIDS patients who are no longer able to shop or to prepare food for themselves. In each of them the City as Dwelling Place shows through. The tradition of handing the fruits of spirituality to others—*Contemplata aliis tradere*—continues. For besides being themselves, these women are Everywoman; at the very least they challenge all women to find ways to make their spirituality a gift handed on to others.

Home

One of the most interesting, and most evident, truths concerning women's lives is how few stories we have of women who never left home. Even in our fairy tales, a girl is often taken away, or must go away if she is to find her destiny. Yet the truth of many women's lives is, and always has been, that our lives have been centered on home and at home. Many of us never leave home—or else we go from the home of our parents to the home we create with a husband and children. What might we learn about spirituality from all of this?

My guess is that, at least in part, the absence of stories of women at home has profoundly affected what we think of as spirituality. For if we study common understandings of spirituality, we find the predominant image is not remaining at home and Dwelling; the predominant image is *going out, going forth, journeying, going on a quest.* One single step, Dis-Covering, becomes an entire spirituality. Put even more directly, the Dwelling Places traditionally offered have been given to us out of the lives and experiences and psychologies of men.

Therefore spirituality as a whole, for women as well as for men, has remained incomplete because it has not been founded on the lives of all human beings. Especially where Dwelling is concerned, Spirituality has not been created with thought of the lives and experiences of women at home. And so the question can be put even more directly: What might the study of Home, as women who have typically and traditionally remained at home know it, tell all women about our own spirituality? The answer I propose: Home reveals a Dwelling Place that teaches ritual, care, and community.

In one view, working at home is considered dreary, disheartening drudgery. "Who would want to do it?" some ask. The answer appears to be "millions," and that raises the further question whether those who say, "I *want* to do it," know something that others don't. I am not talking of the true drudgery that faces a woman who has worked all day at another job, or cleaning someone else's house, and then comes home to do her own without any help. I am talking instead of those women who engage in daily rituals of making meals, making beds, cleaning rooms, decorating, bathing babies, food shopping, and who enjoy those rituals. I am talking of those women for whom homemaking is their work here on earth.

Kathryn Rabuzzi, a woman who has given much thought to this question, points out that in the case of women's traditional work, the business of housewifery is generally celebrated for its purposeful and productive side. But, she says, when we look at housework as having merit on its own instead of as some kind of "production," we then start to see the presence of ritual. And rituals are actions performed with regular rhythm, just as priests perform sacred acts. A woman engaging regularly in these rhythms finds that she shapes the rhythm, and in turn the rhythm shapes her. The woman working at home is sister to the woman planting and tending a Garden, who in turn finds herself planted and tended. Her daily actions, done in rhythm and ritual instead of routine, create a harmony between her inner and outer worlds. Even if she has not consciously recognized it, a woman who chooses to do housework may make this choice because it helps her to understand who she is.

And of course what this can teach all women is the need in each of our lives for pattern, ritual, routine, and the healing power of daily rhythms. If we look at the differences in serenity in an old couple—he with little or no sense of worth because he has "retired," she continually refreshed by the rhythms of her life, built up over a lifetime—we can learn some of the grace of these rhythms. Without such patterns and rhythms a woman can be scattered, diffused, un-centered. With them, she can have a base, a *home* base. Home, as Dwelling Place, is the place she—and we—become centered through the actions of ritual.

But Home is also the place for learning care, and the "thicker times" of presence which care teaches. "Thicker times," Rabuzzi tells us, "are what consistently fill the caretaker's life with dread. A back turned for just an instant can occasion irreversible damage, even death. The back door of a fourth-floor apartment momentarily left unlatched and a toddling two-year-old wanders out onto the unscreened fire escape; the spaghetti pot of boiling water left unwatched for just the moment it takes to walk across the floor to the phone; the Drano accidentally set under the bathroom sink instead of in the locked cabinet."

And yet thicker times, in addition to teaching dread, also give women awareness of the fundamental need human beings have to care for one another, especially for the essential and inviolable sacredness of child care. And when care becomes understood in this thicker sense, the Home also reveals the need all women have for the care of others. For if a Home is an ideal or complete place, it is a setting where a woman not only *gives* care; it is also a setting where a woman *receives* care. Every woman needs to face this need for care, Dwelling Place, and Home; to accept it when it is offered; and to ask for it when it is not.

Finally, more than any other Dwelling Place, Home is the place for entering human community—spirituality not only as being-*there*, but also as being-*with*. Home is the place where loneliness can be relieved through community, which is one profound meaning of the too-often trivialized coffee klatch. It is also the place where homelessness can be understood in its truly heartbreaking dimension—by considering exactly what the *absence* of home means. Home is generally the place for lovemaking, and even more, for people-making, often for as long as eighteen years. Sometimes it can be for much longer—think for a moment of the homemaking of mothers of children with special needs. And for those who search beneath its many layers of meaning, as we are trying to do here, it eventually becomes clear that the truest meaning of "coming home" is not a coming home to a mother or child, a lover or spouse; it is coming home to ourselves. Being at Home means putting all the masks aside and simply Dwelling in a place where we can be who we are.

Once the masks are put aside, Home as Dwelling Place reveals itself in its deepest dimension: We are Home; we are always *at* Home; and it is at the center of our own being that Mystery dwells. For if Coming Home means coming to oneself, then we ourselves are a Dwelling Place for Mystery. We do not go *out*, in the last analysis, to the Home, just as we do not go out, in the last analysis, to Desert, Garden, or City. Instead, we take each of them with us wherever we go, because we *are* Desert, we *are*

Garden, we *are* City, we *are* Home. Etty Hillesum, the young Jewish woman who died in Auschwitz in 1943, and who left us her diary, wrote that she had learned in the last two years of her life: "We *are* 'at home.' Under the sky. In every place on earth, if only we carry everything within us . . . *We must be our own country.*" When we discover that, the capacity for Dwelling, wherever we are, becomes ours.

With Whom Do We Dwell?

Dwelling means place, presence, rest—and we live out this dwelling not only in actual places but, at a deeper level, in symbolic, centering spiritual locations which turn out to be within ourselves. Still, there is one final question at the Station of Dwelling. Who are our companions in dwelling? With whom do we dwell?

We Dwell with Ourselves

So far throughout this book, in at least one practice of each chapter we concentrate on our senses. That assumes a first companion with whom we dwell—ourselves. Perhaps more significantly, we dwell in companionship with our bodies, our physical selves. Certain practices of spirituality have traditionally addressed the body, especially actions such as bowing and bending—"When true simplicity is gained, to *bow* and to *bend* we will not be ashamed" goes the old Shaker hymn—walking in processions, dancing, kneeling, kissing, joining hands in prayer, even lying prostrate on the ground. The body expresses outwardly what the spirit is doing within. But our senses companion us in a special way: our *sight* brings awareness of beauty in our midst; our *hearing* attunes us to sound as well as to silence; and our *touch* is perhaps the most powerful medium we possess for expressing healing, compassion, and love, whether toward another human being or toward the nonhuman creation surrounding us.

We Dwell with Other Creatures

A second set of companions with whom we dwell is that entire universe of things—living and nonliving elements in the universe that enable us to dwell as physical spiritual beings. Water, earth, fire, and air are perhaps the most noticeable—literally we cannot live without them—but so too are wood and wine, sand and stone, birds, bugs, and butterflies. In a very special place is our companionship with the nonhuman animals: dogs, cats, horses, chickens, and squirrels. Children have no difficulty realizing that clouds are God's thoughts, as are hills and moonlight and the less obvious companions of our earthly dwelling. Walt Whitman knew this possibility and wrote in *Leaves of Grass* about the child who went forth every day and the first object she looked upon, that object she became. He wrote about the child *in us* who still goes forth every day, and will always go forth every day.

The child in each of us is the child who sees this and knows the secret (even if she has temporarily forgotten it) that we are in communion with everything that is. Learning to contemplate everything around us, come to communion with it, get inside it, and even become it helps us not only in the physical *practice* of Dwelling, but in the *attitude* as well.

We Dwell with Other People

Still, one set of companions stands out in our dwelling more than any other: the human beings with whom we share life, death, and all that comes between. As I have already noted, a spirituality that is only about ourselves or only about God, for that matter, is aborted and stunted spirituality. To flourish spiritually we need to engage in a continual dancing toward a common sisterhood/brotherhood with all people—with human beings everywhere. We can be helped to this by engaging in practices of spirituality not only alone, but together; by experiencing ourselves as part of spiritual communities in our homes, places of work, places of worship, travel, shopping—in our deserts and gardens and cities. We can also lean on the spiritual strengths of others by asking for their support as we try to develop our own.

One of the simplest ways of doing this is to take part in prayers of companionship. One I have often used begins with our sitting in a circle and recalling that we are Dwelling in the Presence of Mystery. Together we have then prayed the "Prayer of the Single Word." Instead of asking each of those present to speak a long prayer, or offer extensive comment, each person in the circle is asked to choose one word to sum up her prayer and then share the word out loud. Women to whom I have taught this prayer often tell me they in turn have taught it to others—sometimes asking those present to choose a theme, such as the name of a person who is ill (and so the words: "Mary, Jessie, Helen, Louise, Nancy, Kit, Tom . . ." in each case allowing for a few moments of silence after each word);

a country that is troubled (and so the words: "Iran, South Africa, Ireland, Lebanon, Cameroon . . ."); a grace or gift that is desired (and so the words: "peace, sobriety, hope, health, love, money, wisdom . . ."). A practice such as this, done corporately and in community, teaches us more than any sermon does that we are not alone in our spirituality: We dwell together with others, or we do not dwell at all.

We Dwell with God

And finally, there is one last companion in dwelling. We dwell in the company of the Holy One. Dwelling with God makes Dwelling with anything or anyone else possible. Dwelling with God is the blood and bone and sinew and skeleton of all companionship—the Companionship of all companionship.

Often in this book we speak of that Holy One as the Mystery at the heart of all. Some of us, in living out our spiritual lives, speak directly to this Mystery; others of us do not address it at all and are content to let it approach us on its own terms and in its own time. Some of us call this Mystery by name: Father, Mother, God, Lady Wisdom, Creator Spirit, Yahweh. Others of us feel uncomfortable with such names, especially if they are exclusively male, and are searching for new ones. And still others of us feel it profound blasphemy to give *any* name to the One who would appear to be essentially beyond all human naming. I once taught a class of women who wanted to include a ritual of spirituality in each class session, but they could come to no agreement about the One they wanted to address as part of the ritual. They finally compromised by speaking of "the Unnameable"—and that seemed to me an insightful and deeply spiritual compromise.

Nevertheless, because many, perhaps most, women feel that Spirituality is a way of life where we are engaged in *Awakening, Creating,* and *Nourishing* the Communion between ourselves and all that is by *Dis-Covering* the Mystery at the heart of all that is, and *Dwelling* in this Mystery, attention must be paid to the Mystery Who Is the Ground, Depth, and Being of all Companionship. And when no name will do, some have discovered they can engage in Dwelling by addressing the Mystery simply as "Thou." Indeed, for these women, the step of Dwelling begins with "Thou," ends with "Thou," and is sustained throughout a lifetime by the awareness of "Thou."

However, the sustaining—of any of the Steps, but especially of

Dwelling—does not just happen. Instead it is a result of many steps of spirituality learned throughout life and engaged in throughout the seasons. Dwelling will wither and wind down if we do not look after it. It needs to be nourished or it will be in danger of death. We move, therefore, to the next Step, examining some of the spiritual sources of support and vitality that keep Dwelling alive and enable our spirituality to flourish. For we have now arrived at the fifth Step, the Step of Nourishing.

The Practice of Dwelling

The seven practices of Dwelling are opportunities to engage in, as well as to deepen, the Dwelling that already exists in your spirituality. Ideally, you should practice at least one of them every day, giving yourself a full complement of fifteen or twenty minutes (which may be divided into parts and also expanded to twice daily, or forty minutes), even if you must rearrange your day. Done consistently, they will become rituals in your life, rituals that have their own rhythms, allowing you to dwell whenever and wherever you choose, as well as making Dwelling a permanent part of your spirituality. The preliminary steps for each practice are to:

 • Sit comfortably and easily, in a quiet place if possible, but on a bus or train if that is necessary.

 • Shut out any outside noise by attentiveness to your inner self.

 • Close your eyes and become attuned to your breathing, to the rhythm and pace of your breath. Be sure to spend—at this Step—at least four minutes coming to awareness of your breathing. Inhale gently; exhale gently. Feel your body coming to a place of rest. For some practices, you will need to open your eyes after these first four minutes; for others, the closing of your eyes is essential. You will discover for yourself for which ones closed—or open—eyes are appropriate.

Practice 1: Dwelling in Your Senses

After closing your eyes, be aware of your eyes as they rest behind your eyelids. Feel them resting in their places. When you have become aware of them, let your capacity for *Seeing* enfold and embrace you so that you are inside your own seeing, so that you are dwelling within your seeing. Become your seeing; rest within it; be present to it; be identified with it, and plan to return to it several times during the coming day.

After closing your eyes, be aware of your ears resting at the sides of your head. Feel them silently in their places. When you have become as aware of them as possible, let your capacity for *Hearing* enfold and embrace you so that you are inside your own hearing, so that you are dwelling within your hearing. Become your hearing; rest within it; be present to it; be identified with it; listen to it, and plan to return to abiding within your hearing several times during the coming day.

After closing your eyes, be aware of your mouth, and of your tongue, your teeth, and the inside of your mouth. Feel them silently in their places. When you have become as aware of them as possible, let your capacity for *Tasting* enfold and embrace you so that you are inside your own tasting, so that you are dwelling within your tasting. Become your tasting; rest within it; be present to it; be identified with it; listen to it, and plan to return to abiding within your tasting several times during the coming day.

After closing your eyes, be aware of your nose, and of your nostrils, and the air coming in and being exhaled. Feel your nose as it gently breathes in and out. When you have become as aware of your breathing as possible, let your capacity for *Breathing* enfold and embrace you so that you are inside your own breathing, so that you are dwelling within your breathing. Become your breathing; rest within it; be present to it; be identified with it; listen to it, and plan to return to abiding within your breathing several times during the coming day.

After closing your eyes, be aware of your fingertips, and of the soles of your feet. Feel the surface your fingertips are touching; feel the shoes, or stockings, or surface touching your feet. When you have become as aware of your touching as possible, let your capacity for *Touching* enfold and embrace you so that you are inside your own touching, so that you are dwelling within your touching. Become your touching; rest within it; be present to it; be identified with it; listen to it, and plan to return to abiding within your touching several times during the coming day.

At the end of fifteen or twenty minutes, take another 120 or 180 seconds to be attentive to the rhythm of your breath. Then gently and slowly open your eyes and conclude with either a spoken word or with a gesture to the Mystery within you and all around you as an act of thanksgiving.

You may find, after doing this practice, that you want to concentrate on only one sense and not on all five; or to concentrate on a different sense at a different time during the day. Go with your intuition, your instinct, in all cases. You are the one to decide on the best way to spend these minutes. But try not to spend any *less* than fifteen or twenty minutes, to receive the full benefit of the practice.

Practice 2: Planning for Presence

Read the practice first. Then engage in the three preliminary steps, remembering at this Step to engage in four full minutes of attending to your breath.

At this Step, we read Thich Nhat Hanh's suggestions about washing the dishes. The purpose of this practice is to assist you in planning one or two common practices during the coming day when you will remember to practice presence.

1. Reflect on your daily activities, and choose any two that are common in your life (preparing meals, signing your name, opening letters, turning on a computer or typewriter, waiting in line for a bus or train, kissing your children).

2. Imagine yourself doing the first of these practices during the day ahead. See yourself doing it; see the circumstances, the room, the time, your companions. Say to yourself several times (for example), "Sylvia, when turning on the computer, be aware of turning on the computer . . ." Repeat this in rhythm, following your breath.

3. Imagine yourself doing the second of these practices during the day ahead. See yourself doing it; see the circumstances, the room, the time, your companions. Say to yourself, now, several times (for example), "Lois, when waiting for the bus, be aware of waiting for the bus . . ." Repeat this in rhythm, following your breath.

Conclude this planning practice by breathing silently for at least two minutes.

Practice 3: The Autobiography of Your Dwelling Places

Read the practice first. Then engage in the three preliminary steps.

Draw a time line across the paper, or on a separate page, marking the line at five-year intervals, e.g.:

5	10	15	20	25	30
35	40	45	50	55	60
65	70	75	80	85	90

Above each number, corresponding to that age in your life, write the name of a place that was a dwelling place for you at that time—either an actual place or a symbolic place, such as desert, garden, city, or home.

Below each number, corresponding to that age in your life, write the name of who or what was God for you at that time and in that place.

Note for yourself where and how your dwelling places, and your image of divinity, has changed; and where and how they have remained constant over the years.

When you have completed the time line for both place and divinity, breathe simply—simply breathe—with your eyes closed for at least two minutes.

Then open your eyes to conclude the exercise.

Practice 4: The Desert As Dwelling Place

Read the practice first. Then engage in the three preliminary steps.

This exercise is one where you recall the desert as dwelling place in your life.

Before engaging in the exercise, find some sand—from the beach or from the ground outside. Or, find some stones that will be your companions in this exercise.

1. After the four minutes of breathing, hold the sand or the stones in your hand (or put them in a container and hold it). Look at them quietly, trying to be present to them, as they are present to you. Take time to be with them; do not hurry.

2. In what ways do they represent past desert dwelling places of your life?

3. If this recalling brings feelings of sorrow back to you, stay with these feelings, be present to them, allow them to wash over you.

4. In what ways do they represent present desert dwelling places of your life?

5. Again, if this remembering brings feelings of sorrow, stay with these feelings, be present to them, allow them to wash over you.

6. In what ways are you a desert dwelling place? If so, are there any ways you would choose to change this?

7. Are there any ways in which the Unnameable is a desert dwelling place in your life? If so, be present before this Mystery.

Conclude the practice by sitting silently with the sand or stones for at least two minutes, breathing the desert in and out.

Practice 5: The Garden As Dwelling Place

Read the practice first. Then engage in the three preliminary steps.

This practice requires you to be outside in an actual garden or to look out your window at a garden nearby.

1. After the four minutes of breathing, be present to the Garden and permit it to be present to you.

2. In what way does this garden represent past garden dwelling places in your life?

3. What circumstances or characteristics of past gardens in your life do you want to continue to cultivate? What circumstances or characteristics of past gardens do you want to bring to the present?

4. In what way does this garden represent present garden dwelling places in your life? Try to listen to what this garden tells you.

5. Which present circumstances of garden as dwelling place cause you to rejoice? Which sadden you? Be present to both of these.

6. In what ways are you a Garden for yourself? For others?

7. Are there any ways in which the Unnameable is a Garden in your spirituality? If so, be present before this Mystery.

Conclude this practice by sitting quietly in the garden or looking quietly out the window for at least two minutes, breathing the garden in and out, and allowing it to breathe you in return.

Practice 6: The City As Dwelling Place

Read the practice first. Then, before doing the first step, engage in the three preliminary steps.

The City is the traditional place for works of mercy: feeding the hungry, giving drink to the thirsty, sheltering the homeless, clothing the naked, visiting the imprisoned—in hospitals or in homebound circles or in actual prisons—caring for the sick, and burying the dead. In this practice, you are to choose to do one of these activities on a volunteer basis for at least three hours each week.

1. Contact a person or an agency in your neighborhood that is engaged in one of the works of mercy.

2. Ask what you might do as a volunteer for three hours a week.

3. Make a commitment to this volunteer work for a period of at least three months.

4. Keep a brief journal of diary entries about this work and its impact upon you.

5. Engage at least one other person to go with you to the City as Dwelling Place.

Each time you engage in this practice, both before you go and after you return, engage in at least fifteen minutes of breathing. You may wish to use the mantra, "The City is my Dwelling Place," or you may wish to begin and end with a silent fifteen-minute period.

Practice 7: Home As Dwelling Place

Read the practice first. Then engage in the three preliminary steps.

Home is a Dwelling Place for ritual, care, and community. It is also a place we *are* for others, and others are for us. This practice is an opportunity to explore each of these in our own lives.

After the four minutes of breathing, you are asked to dwell with your reflections and responses to each of the following questions for at least two or three minutes.

1. What ritual that you do in the home helps to "pattern" you, to make you more who you are?

2. Whom do you care for in your home? Who in your home cares for you? Which is more difficult, and why?

3. Is Home for you the same as your own dwelling place, or do you find it elsewhere? Does the presence of the people you consider your closest community have anything to do with your answer?

4. Say to your body, "You are my Home." Repeat the phrase several times, allowing its truth to enter you and you to enter it. What happens when you dwell with this phrase?

5. To what things in the nonhuman world (bread, wine, stars, air . . .) do you say, "You are my home"? Do they say this to you in return?

6. To what people do you say, "You are my home"? Do they say this to you in return?

7. Do you ever pray to the divinity, the Unnameable as Home? Can you repeat the prayer "You are my Home" to this Mystery? If you can, do so now, gently and quietly, in rhythm with your breathing.

Conclude the practice with two minutes of breathing where you simply repeat the word "Home . . . Home . . . Home" as a mantra.

5
Nourishing

A Pause for Centering

Let us begin by being still. Sit back in your spirit; do that by sitting back in your body. This Fifth Step is Nourishing. Let your own reflections on Nourishing emerge from your inner self. Take time, don't hurry, and try to spend at least a few moments with each question. Do the same with each of your responses.

Have you ever prayed regularly?

Do you pray now?

If you do pray, why and for what do you pray?

Have you ever fasted for a spiritual reason, in contrast to dieting to lose weight? If you have, what was the reason? What was the result? How did fasting make you feel?

Have you ever consciously tried to practice new behavior, new ways of thinking and acting? Especially, have you ever consciously tried to develop interior gifts such as patience, serenity, or mindfulness?

Did you find it easy or difficult?

What helped you, and what held you back, as you tried a new activity? Can you recall an incident where you suddenly realized you were more patient, more serene, or more mindful?

Do you think of spirituality as something a person engages in individually? Or do you think of it as also being the work of a community of people—a church or temple or some other organized group—who come together to deepen their lives?

Have you ever created a ritual for a special occasion in someone's life? For one in your own? If you did, what was the occasion? What kind of ritual did you create?

What is your favorite among your ordinary, daily rituals? Why?

Are you aware of the poor, the hungry, and the homeless around you? If you are, do you engage in any direct and practical work to lessen their sufferings?

Do you try to nourish and feed your spirituality by giving it a regular diet of practices and exercises, just as you feed your body? If not, would you like to see what is involved in such feeding, and perhaps try some of it out?

The first time I taught a course on spirituality, I suggested the participants make a commitment to engage regularly in some definite practice. "Decide on a weekly set of disciplines," I said, giving them a list, "which includes at least three of the following:

- Twenty minutes of daily prayer, meditation, contemplation, or silent stillness

- One day a week where you don't use a car

- One day a week where you go without one meal

- One day a week with three or four hours of service to others

- Fifteen minutes of journal writing at least three times a week

- One day a week of genuine Sabbath."

An alternate to that requirement was "Decide on a weekly spiritual discipline based on the above, but agree with a group of three to five people to come together every week to reflect on each one's practice."

The response was almost universally positive. For one thing, they had signed up for the course. But the requirement also had the positive effect of giving "permission" to very busy people to do something they really *wanted* to do; these were mostly adults, in their twenties through fifties, who were part-time students, juggling work and family and school, wishing they had some time to just *be,* but also feeling a bit guilty about that wish. So the requirement "took" and one outcome was that people discovered innumerable other activities that were right for them besides the ones I'd listed. Their discoveries covered a wide range: the Buddhist practice of the half-smile several times a day when they wanted to "collect" themselves; the rhythmic and meditative quality of regular running/jogging; the ancient art of Centering.

Others discovered their lives enriched when they prayed regularly with others. "We are *con-spiring* with one another!" one woman suddenly realized after we had concluded our regular opening meditation together as a class. And still another participant, summing up her experience at the end, wrote:

> At the beginning of the semester, I committed myself to the following disciplines: twenty minutes daily prayer/meditation, thirty minutes walking at least three times a week, staying away from between-meal snacks and from any food with sugar, and weekly meetings with a prayer support group. The walking was the time I most experienced the connectedness between my body and spirit. The abstinence and service have been regular parts of my spiritual discipline for some time now—so long that I had forgotten to think of their spiritual basis anymore. The small group was perhaps the most beneficial experience of all. It provided both support for and insight into my personal quiet times.

And another woman told me:

> Discipline helps snap me back to the present moment. It provides a framework that channels and directs my creative energy. For example, the discipline of fasting increases my compassion for the hunger pangs of millions of others as well as focusing my attention on my own neediness and weakness, and ultimately on my dependence for everything on God or God/dess.

My intention in setting that requirement was similar to my intention in this chapter: to explore some of the many practices of spirituality and to suggest the support that comes from working with others as well as offering a repertoire of dance steps appropriate for people of different dispositions and needs. But the fundamental reason for the requirement is this: *The spiritual life needs Nourishing.* It needs a regular program of health maintenance, exercise, and calisthenics, just as our bodies do. Otherwise, as noted in the Step of Dwelling, we wind down, and a kind of aridity sets in as the reminder that periodically we must pause to take nourishment. Without Nourishing, we contract a dry skin of the soul.

In this chapter we examine ten of the sources of this nourishment. All have a long history as practices or, to use the more conventional term, "disciplines"; and for centuries, in Eastern and Western religious traditions, members of these traditions have been taught these ways in one form or another. Many of the practices we have already considered in this book provide specific examples.

However, in this chapter we stand back and look at what we have been doing, not only in more detail but also in ways that are more general and explanatory. If we are regularly doing the practices, we will undoubtedly feel comfortable and familiar with much that is here. Nonetheless, the particular angle of vision at this step will be novel in at least three ways.

First, we will come to these practices/disciplines as women. Second, we will insist on at least three elements: the *personal,* the *communal,* and the *integrating.* We will see out of our own experience that Nourishing is incomplete without all three—genuine spirituality must be *personal* and *communal* and in the direction of *integration.* And third, we will be situating Nourishing in the entire rhythm of spirituality as we have addressed it so far: as sister and companion following on *Awakening, Dis-Covering, Creating,* and *Dwelling,* leading toward *Traditioning* and *Transforming,* and giving life to them all.

A brief word first about *personal, communal,* and *integrating.* We will be examining three *personal* disciplines—prayer, contemplation, and fasting; three *communal* disciplines—liturgy, service, and prophetic speech; and three *integrating* disciplines which overcome division and brokenness—embodiment, memory, and justice. We will also attend to one overarching discipline, *Adoration,* which permeates them all. Of course many more could be named, and this list is not assumed to be exhaustive. It is meant to be a suggestive and definite core—yet even a cursory reading of the names of these ten indicates connections across the lines of personal, communal, and integrating.

Prayer, for example, can be done alone or with others, and it can also be a means of integrating body and spirit. *Prophetic speech* can be uttered by one person or by a group of people, and it can be a powerful source of ending divisions, or integrating. Attending to *Memory* can be a solitary activity between a woman and the Source of Being or a community activity between several people, which brings together past and present. Obviously, there are no hard-and-fast boundaries. Nonetheless, it is also true that the point of departure for each discipline is slightly different, as is its emphasis and its focus. Having said this, let us examine each of the disciplines, personal, communal, and integrating, in detail.

Personal Disciplines

Prayer

Prayer is so central to spirituality that the two are often made synonymous. Prayer basically means request, petition, or entreaty, but often—especially in the presence of the Holy—it expands to include praise, thanksgiving, and our expression of sorrow over the failures and the evil in our lives. Generally, and appropriately, prayer is addressed to God, to the One we call the Unnameable, Father, Mother, Goddess, or simply "Thou." For some of us, only a few words are needed to pray: a repetition, for example, of "Thou . . . Thou . . . Thou . . ." acknowledging ourselves in the presence of the Other.

Others of us pray best by using set formulas, often learned from our own religious traditions: "The Lord is my Shepherd, I shall not want . . ." or "Our Father, who art in heaven . . ." or "Blessed art Thou, O Lord our God, Ruler of the Universe." For still others, prayer to the Holy One is only prayer when it is spontaneous, and many women grow up being quite at ease praying with whatever words come to mind, creating their own prayers, as this woman does:

TO THE GODDESS

Let me know thee better,
O cradle of my youth,
Source of my plenty,
Cool wooded retreat for my sorrow,

and soft bed for my final sleep—
my first and last Mother.

Taking time to pray to the Divinity, no matter how we address that One, is helped immeasurably by two companion disciplines, *Breathing* and *Centering*. Of breathing, the story is told of a beginner who approached a Hindu teacher for initiation into the art of prayer. The teacher said, "Concentrate on your breathing." The petitioner did exactly that for about five minutes. At that point, the teacher said, "The air you breathe is God. You are breathing God in and out. Become aware of that and stay with that awareness." The petitioner followed these instructions each day, sometimes for hours, and discovered a wisdom that held firm for a lifetime: Prayer is not a difficult, secret activity available only to chosen initiates—it is as simple as breathing.

The practice of *Centering* has a similar simplicity: The procedure begins with our sitting relaxed and quiet, and attempting to become aware of our own inner calm, as we have been doing for the quiet reflection at the beginning of each Step. For a few moments, you simply wait on the Presence within you and around you, and after a time—although this is not to be forced—a single word may emerge: "yes," "no," "pain," "peace," "now."

Repeating the word slowly and effortlessly helps you move into a deeper serenity and mindfulness, allowing the Mystery at the Center of all that is to enfold you. I know many women and men who use this practice at least once or twice daily. Engaged in regularly, it nourishes a fuller inner life.

But prayer may also be addressed to other people, and even to the nonhuman world. In ordinary speech, we say regularly to each other, "Pray that I . . ." or "I pray you to . . ."—we pray to each other. And it is not unusual to pray to people who were close to us who have died. The story is told of a thirteen-year-old girl in Belfast, whose little sister had been killed accidentally in a bombing, and whose entire family was in terrible distress. Asked, "And do you pray to God about all this?" she answered, "Not always. But I do pray to my sister." As for the nonhuman world, the ancient Hebrew psalms often address creation directly, suggesting perhaps that we do the same: "Praise God, sun and moon, praise God all you shining stars. Praise God, you highest heavens . . . you mountains and all you hills . . . you wild beasts and all tame animals." (Ps. 148: 3, 4a, 9, 10)

Contemplation

At some point in our childhood, many of us had the experience of sitting quietly with a magnifying glass, holding it motionless in order to catch the sun in a still, concentrated point on a piece of paper. If we were centered and patient enough, and amazingly could learn to *do nothing,* the paper ignited—the sun connected and the fire began. We had found a sun-filled center. This was, and is, *contemplation,* letting go and letting be in an act of concentration so total we are able to hold the Sun. For some of us, this is also a form of prayer—contemplative prayer—just as prayer can be a form of contemplation—prayerful contemplation—and not really a separate discipline.

I think of two women I know: one, Ruth, stopped to see me last week on her way home to Zurich. She is seven months' pregnant with her first child, and as we spoke of the coming birth, she placed her hand on her belly and said, "I can feel this life, I can feel it moving within me—and yet, I cannot talk of it—the mystery, the continuing wonder and surprise of the life simply being here is beyond my words." This too is contemplation.

The other woman is my sister-in-law Dotty, sitting across from me in the early evening. Her infant daughter is at her breast, feeding. But it is Dotty who is aware of Nourishing. In giving life to Jennifer, her face is transformed and her whole being involved. Sitting there, in contemplative stillness, with every sense focused on the infant, like the magnifying glass, she catches the sun. In one sense, she is really not with *me* at all. But in another sense, she is *more* with me, and indeed with all that exists, because the feeding places her at the center of the Mystery, enabling her to dwell there. This too is contemplation.

And what all three—the child with the glass, the pregnant young woman, the nursing mother—have in common is their possession of the essence of contemplation. They have achieved a stillness, without actively seeking the stillness; they are in communion with the Mystery by allowing the Mystery to enfold them. They are fully alive in every sense—and yet beyond all sense experience as we know it. They have passed into a country of the spirit where Awakening and Dis-Covering and Creating and Dwelling are fused. They reside in the heart of the Mystery which Itself resides at the center of everything that is.

To become proficient in the discipline of Contemplation, we must be willing to live in the midst of paradox. For we can only know the

Mystery by letting go of knowing, and by putting aside our reason, our thinking, our too quick words. We must sit still, doing nothing at all. We must wait, as we did at the Step of Creating where contemplation began the process, allowing things to reveal themselves to us, and seek by allowing ourselves to be sought. In contemplation we must take *Thou* in by allowing ourselves to be taken in. By doing these things, we will gradually become "modern" contemplatives and find ourselves living at the still point of the turning world.

Fasting

It is a paradox that fasting is a form of nourishing; still, the discipline of Fasting is the third personal discipline. Some think of fasting as doing harm to themselves, because it includes withdrawing from food and drink for specific periods of time. But when I suggest it here my intention is not self-denial—many women are already too good at that. Instead, I want to offer an opportunity to see what happens when we break familiar patterns. For when we fast, we disrupt the normal order of regular meals and set routine. And that in turn—as illustrated by the quotes from the women on p. 116—has other, unexpected effects such as an awareness of hunger in our own neighborhoods; an awareness of ways we engage in unexamined self-abuse through food and especially drink; an awareness of how we allow routine to control us; and an awareness of our relation to time.

Further possibilities for fasting exist, however, in areas not always thought of as appropriate to fasting, where we abstain not just from food, but from other regular, unexamined habits. Just as fasting for one meal a day, or even for one day a week, can alert us to our relation to our bodies, fasting in the broader sense can enrich us spiritually, enabling us to *see* ourselves and our world from other perspectives. Three of the more practical forms for our modern lives are fasting from *television*, fasting from the *car*, and fasting from *shopping*.

Many of us remember the practice of "giving up" something for Lent. Fasting is such a giving up, not to inflict pain on ourselves, but to help ourselves consider other and more active ways to be and to see life from other perspectives. Instead of watching television, we might, for example, call on neighbors or friends who are shut-ins, take long walks, or plant a garden. We might begin keeping a journal. Or, like one woman I know, we might decide to relearn the practice of letter writing in the evening, instead of being a "couch potato," and revive a faithful and fruitful correspondence with friends.

Other women, who habitually jump in the car for everything, instead of walking, notice that when they fast from the car—even for one day—they *see* differently: They notice leaves on the ground, or the look of a blade of grass, or the face of another person passing on the street. Still others, addicted to shopping although not in any need, discover *genuine* human need around them when they no longer treat the mall as a place of worship. For each of these fastings, the outcome is the same as it is when fasting from food and drink—a new sense of self, a new sense of time, and a new vision of possibilities in spirituality.

Communal Disciplines

Liturgy

Liturgy is the traditional name given to people coming together with the intention of praying and worshipping in *communion* and *community*. The word "Liturgy" means the "work of the people," acting as a reminder that one of our most important works is to praise our Creator *together* and to Dwell with one another in a prayerful manner. But Liturgy also means "service"—"waiting upon" the Holy One in both senses—and so comes the phrase "worship service." Liturgy is communal, not privatized, and it involves a set form, specific procedures, or, to use a religious term, *ritual.*

The first point to make about Liturgy is that its focus is the Other—the Holy, the Beyond in our Midst, the Inexpressible Mystery. If spirituality is communion with and dwelling in this Mystery, then we need opportunities to come together and celebrate our common presence in the midst of this Mystery. In other words, we *need* rituals, and we *need* liturgy. Historically, however, women have not been participants in the creation of religious rituals and our experience has been excluded as the focus of liturgy. Women have not, until very recently, and only in some religious groups, been permitted to be leaders of liturgy. And so the practice is one where we are more likely to be spectators than active participants.

We can continue to be passive spectators in the many liturgies and rituals of our lives. But for a complete spirituality, a better route is the creation of rituals and liturgies that *do* include us, *do* speak for us, and *do* place us in the position of celebrants and full participants in the community work of acknowledging the continuing Presence of the Goodness gifting our lives. Thus, the particular practice of liturgy for women today is the creation of our own rituals.

Women are already doing this around the world. And although we have done so for centuries on a small scale, today such creating is widespread. The last twenty years have seen a resurgence of ritual-creating on the part of women, and these rituals clue us in to some fundamental possibilities. First are the rituals where we celebrate the presence of Mystery at the center of creation, focusing on a meal or some material element such as water, milk, or soil, and doing that from women's perspectives. I have, for example, been part of a women's ritual meal several times, where we built on Judy Chicago's artwork in *The Dinner Party* by preparing place mats for our foremothers or for forgotten women in our traditions, as she does. After we had done that, we gathered in groups at the place prepared and toasted the lives of these women. I have taken part in toasts to Medea, to Ruth and Naomi, to Anne Frank, and to women whose names I had never heard before, as well as to the Mystery at the center of these lives. One such remembrance was of a twenty-five-year-old nurse friend of one of the women, who had been raped and killed the week before. A group of strangers when we began, we stood in shared sisterhood during those moments.

I know, too, of a ritual meal that includes the blessing of wine where seven women bless the cup in seven different languages, beginning in Hebrew with the core blessing of the Jewish tradition and passing the cup around the circle: *"Brucha ya Shechinah, malcha ha alam Baray pri ha' gafen"* ("Blessed are you, Shechinah, Queen of the Universe, who has brought forth the fruit of the vine").

In addition, I know of rituals celebrating the earth—common living dirt—and milk, the great female symbol of Nourishing, where in the sharing and blessing of the milk women are invited to name and tell stories of the women who have nourished them, and to pour milk from a pitcher into a cup at the bottom of which are cinnamon and other sweet spices.

Another set of rituals are those addressing critical times and crises known only to women, especially first menstruation. One woman told me of being taken out to dinner by her mother and grandmother at the time of her first period for a celebratory meal, a ritual that served both to confirm her new sense of womanhood and allay her fears of this not yet completely understood occurrence. Women have recently developed rituals that acknowledge other times of Awakening, be it giving form to their feelings about divorce, widowhood, abortion, the birth of a child, or the death of a parent. Others take time to create and then take part in rituals for saying goodbye, ending close relationships, or celebrating fiftieth birthdays. There are also rituals of *healing* after wife battering and of *silence-breaking* about incest or rape. And when these rituals are done in community, they invariably give support, strength, and the ability to live more deeply to the women who are the focus, as well as to those who participate.

A final set of rituals are those developed in traditional religious communities, where the ritual for the female needs some changing; where one cannot simply adapt a ritual prepared for men to women. Many sensitive men are willing to help in the re-creation. These also include rituals that eliminate negative or destructive assumptions—including the words of some prayers—concerning girls and women. Naomi Janowitz and Maggie Wenig have written Sabbath prayers for women; Judith Plaskow has prepared a ceremony for bringing a daughter into the Jewish Covenant; and Aviva Cantor has written a "Jewish Women's Haggadah." Rebecca Parker and Joanne Brown have created a coming-out ritual for lesbian women. And Christian women are re-creating sacramental rituals so they are more appropriate to their own experience, from the rituals of Reconciliation, Eucharist, and Baptism to Marriage and Ordination. In doing so, they are creating and contributing to a new spirituality which serves to nourish the spiritual lives of women throughout the world.

Service

At the step of Dwelling, I noted the belief that because we are unlimited in imagination and because of our ability to dream—we have *a capacity for the universe*. I also said that if we don't exercise this capacity, we become narrow and shriveled. The fruits of spirituality ripen when given to others. The translation into daily life of this capacity for the universe is its embodiment in service. A description as old as the meaning of this spiritual discipline comes from the prophet Isaiah, speaking for God:

> Is not this the fast that I choose: to loose the bonds
> of wickedness, to undo the thongs of the yoke, to let
> the oppressed go free, and to break every yoke?
>
> Is it not to share your bread with the hungry, and
> bring the homeless poor into your house;

when you see the naked, to cover (her) and not to hide
yourself from your own flesh?

Then shall your light break forth like the dawn, and
your healing spring up speedily;

your righteousness shall go before you, the glory of
the Lord shall be your rear guard.

Then you shall call, and the Lord will answer;

You shall cry, and (God) will say, "Here I am."
(Is. 58:6–9)

Service as a discipline and as a practice in spirituality takes three
forms. The first is direct relief to those who are suffering or in need,
making sure to include ourselves. Such service ranges from volunteering on
a regular basis to answering hot lines dealing with suicide and drugs, to
regular participation in washing dishes or serving meals at soup kitchens, to
visiting the elderly or shut-ins, to shopping for those who are housebound,
to reading to the blind, to treating ourselves to a hot bath when we are
exhausted. It includes working in hospitals and hospices, in refugee camps,
in detention centers, in prisons. It also includes offering our gifts through
teaching English as a second language, knitting, gardening, sewing, driving, cooking, and CPR. In teaching Spirituality, as I have already noted, I
suggest that women take part once a week in some form of such service.
Many times, they do not have to add anything to their daily lives; the
suggestion brings to light service they are already offering—at home,
perhaps, caring for a sick or elderly parent.

The second form, although still direct, occurs at another level.
Here, the service element in a woman's spirituality is practiced by her
working to alleviate the *causes* and the *symptoms* of suffering. Examples of
this kind of service are involvement in community agencies. This includes
seeking to change or get rid of legislation that is unjust, organizing committees
of people to deal with inadequate housing, fund-raising, direct support of
people or agencies who work with the needy, signing public statements, writing
leaflets, pamphlets, and books. Concerts or benefits are often powerful
forms of such service, as we know from Band-Aid, Live-Aid, and Farm-Aid
and hundreds of thousands of women in our country are involved this way.

The third form of service resides in an attitude. The point of view
that sees all human beings—and animals and earth too—as sister and
brother is also a form of service. So too is the willingness to stop and give

directions to a stranger, the giving of a cup of coffee in the Name of the Mystery, the placing of our own concerns on hold for the time being in order to help someone far more in need than ourselves. If we look, we notice these are daily—perhaps hourly—invitations, sometimes accepted, sometimes passed by. With the caution that we not feel guilty when we do not accept each invitation of this kind that occurs, I would still argue this third vision of service as attitude makes the practice of this discipline open to everyone—the bedridden patient, the poorest of the poor, the busiest of the busy, as well as the richest of the rich.

Two warnings about service, however, need to be made to alert the woman who wishes to practice a complete spirituality. First, the word itself is very close to *servant*, and not that far from *slave*. And being a servant or a slave to another is *not* full participation in the Mystery at the center, because it does not serve another to *let* them use us, and certainly is no service to ourselves. In other words, the emphasis on *service* must be just that: an emphasis on work that is done freely, independently, and out of an impulse to help someone in need.

The other warning concerns the difficulty service often appears to be, the stumbling block it offers in many spiritual lives. Too many of us have become used to our own needs and desires—so much so that those of others get forgotten. The notion that spirituality is private dies hard, at least in much of the North American world. But the discipline of Service is there to remind us that we approach the Mystery at the Center of all that is *together* or we do not approach It at all. Service provides a litmus test for whether our spirituality is genuine.

Prophetic Speech

The two communal disciplines just described have Greek as well as English names: *leitourgia*, "liturgy," and *diakonia*, "service," from which we get the English word "deaconess." One more remains, *kerygma*: speech uttered from profound religious conviction. The particularity of the speech I want to describe here, however, lies not in its being just *any* religious speech. Instead, it is speaking, a *prophetic* speaking, in the face of evil, that says loudly, forcefully, and absolutely, "No!"

One meaning of prophecy is the ability to tell the future. That is not the meaning intended here. Instead, I use prophecy, and the word "prophetic," as the Hebrew Bible does and as we did at the Step of Creating. The Hebrew prophets were women and men who had come face-to-face with a God of justice, Who felt sorrow and pathos over the human condition. And these original prophets spoke the word of this grieving God, providing a model for others who attempt to do that today.

Rabbi Abraham Heschel describes prophets as people who give speeches about widows and orphans and the corruption of judges instead of dealing with timeless issues such as being, becoming, philosophy, and wisdom. True prophets aren't interested in tours through the elegant mansions of the mind; their mission is to take us to the slums so that we can get some sense of the actual *faces* of human suffering. And they do that by speaking, using a specific and direct language which is, according to the Rabbi, ". . . the voice that God has lent to the silent agony, to the plundered poor, to the profaned riches of the world." The voice is not the prophet's, however, nor is it our own. For it is God who rages in prophetic voices, and when one of those voices is ours, it is God's voice raging *in us*.

Prophets are often unpopular people, and in the Third Step we discussed how uncomfortable they make many of us. Nevertheless, as with service, prophetic speech is essential to a complete spirituality. Silence in the face of evil, allowing the false word to pass, is corrosive and deadly not only to the victim, but also to the *bystander*. Such silence corrupts not only our world, but also us and our spirituality. There are some realities to which we *must* speak. And we must speak our words in community with one another.

I think the prophetic spirit can be found today in one question that illuminates all the others: "What about the children?" The first person I heard asking that question was Molly Rush, mother of six, grandmother of two, and director of the Thomas Merton Peace Center in Pittsburgh. Because of her directorship she was often asked to join community efforts and demonstrations protesting the proliferation of nuclear arms, nuclear warheads, nuclear missiles, and nuclear submarines—the whole array of lethal weapons our society has created. And her response was always the same. She would think of her family of six and say, "I'm sorry; I can't go with you—*what about the children?*" But one day she heard her own question with reference not to the time given for the protest, but with reference to the impact of the weapons and what they could mean for her own children and the children of the world. And so she began to say no. Publicly. Both in communion and community.

I think also of the mothers and the grandmothers in Buenos Aires, Argentina, in the Plaza de Mayo, arriving day after day for years, holding the pictures of their children and grandchildren—the disappeared ones, the *desaparecidos.* We are told that this group, almost entirely women, was *very* unpopular with Argentinian officials whenever they gathered to ask over and over, "What about the children?" as they still do today. We are also told it was they, more than any group, who were responsible for the end of a reign of terror and torture in Argentina. Again, prophetic speech: in communion and community.

I think of Sadako Sasaki, the child suffering the aftermath of Hiroshima, of whom the story is told that she believed the Japanese proverb that if one made a thousand paper cranes in a lifetime, health would come, but who died of leukemia at ten, before she was finished. The work of making her cranes, however, was continued, and today millions of cranes are flown in many places of the world—but especially by people in Hiroshima on Hiroshima Day, set into the sky by millions of people whose crane making is a way of asking, "What about the children?"

Finally, there is Jean Donovan, one of four church women killed in El Salvador in 1980, who wrote the month before her death, "The Peace Corps left today and my heart sank low. The danger is extreme and they were right to leave . . . Now I must assess my own position, because I am not up for suicide. Several times I have decided to leave. I almost could, except for the children, the poor bruised victims of adult lunacy. Who would care for them? Whose heart would be so staunch as to favor the reasonable thing in a sea of their tears and helplessness? Not mine, dear friend, not mine."

These women teach us that prophetic speech may take many forms: running peace centers, walking silently with others while holding the picture of a child, creating paper cranes, staying at our place for the sake of the small, bruised victims, speaking up at a risk when someone else is the butt of a joke or a snicker or a lie. And the note this sounds in the music of our spirituality is that sometimes it is only through our awareness and sense of the tragic that we enter into the depths of spiritual life.

This is the impact of prophetic speech as a discipline, spoken in community. It arises from our acknowledging the brokenness in life, and from our attending to the agonies of children. But it also arises from the sense of what makes a *complete* spirituality, one that is personal and communal and awake to our call as humans to move toward healing and wholeness. That healing and wholeness are not just our own; they are also the healing and the wholeness we might offer, as women, to a bruised, bent, and broken world.

Which brings us to the last set of Nourishing disciplines, those that are paths for *integration* of body and spirit (Embodiment); of past and present (Memory); and of the good and the not-yet-wholly-good (Justice).

Integrating Disciplines

Embodiment

Giving a workshop in Venice, Florida, I recently sat at a table with three other women. Each of us was naming an activity in our lives that made us feel whole, that nourished our experience of completeness. I named music, both that I performed myself and that I listened to. The woman on my right spoke of walking each evening for an hour. The third woman spoke of writing. And the fourth said she was most complete—and refreshed—when she was able to create and cook a meal for others. It struck me upon reflection that what each had in common was physicality—each of us had described something bodily that made our spirits whole.

Including *embodiment* as a spiritual discipline strengthens several dis-coveries. One is the truth we have already considered that in today's spirituality we find God not by escaping from life, or from our bodies, but in a more complete *involvement* with life. We find God in the *integration* of body and spirit. And that integration ought to have an impact on the moves we make toward healing other historic false divisions. Included are the beliefs that human beings are superior to nonhuman creation; men are superior to women; whites are superior to people of color; rich and literate people are superior to the poor and illiterate, and on and on and on.

Awakening to the pervasiveness of division alerts us to the power in recognizing and cultivating those practices in our lives that at first we may not think of, or realize, as practices of spirituality. These are practices that are bodily in origin, but move in the direction of making us and our societies whole. Those practices may not be *named* as "spiritual," but in actuality they are, for they place us at the center of living and enable us to dwell with wholeness in the Mystery.

As we reflect upon our own lives, as the four of us did, we will undoubtedly be able to name the practices that foster the integration of *our* bodies and spirits. There are things we do regularly that lead us to experience wholeness. Among them are *art*, *sports*, and *sexuality*, each of which is a form of the remaining two.

The fine arts have always been understood to be healing and holistic, and our senses can learn to appreciate music, painting, sculpture, drama, literature, architecture, and dance as well as to take part in them no matter what age we are. However, we need also to take ownership of the bodily work we do which may not immediately strike us as an art: cooking, gardening, typing, nursing, counseling, editing, teaching.

Similarly, sports have always cleared the mind, and a sound mind in a healthy body has been an ideal for centuries. Only in recent years, however, have women been encouraged in sports and physical exercise. And yet, the woman who runs daily tends to be very much in touch not only with the rhythm of her bodily pulse, but with the beat of her spirit as well. The woman who tosses baskets with her children through a hoop on the garage door, or who swims or bikes regularly, also knows the integration of body and spirit.

And finally, because it *is* better to make love than to make war, the loving and passionate practice of sex, the great form of adult play, is perhaps the most bodily of all, and therefore, paradoxically, the most spiritual. For when engaged in with a beloved partner, sex can be the greatest taste we have of ecstasy, delight, wonder, and integration.

Memory

Memory is the spiritual discipline that integrates *Time* for us and brings together past and present. As all good counselors know, assisting people in working through memories, especially painful ones, is critical to integration. Memory as a spiritual discipline is related to this work of listening or *therapy*—a word itself meaning "healing power"—just as it is related to the more ancient discipline of confession. Each of those can lead to the experience of wholeness, because in each instance—listening, therapy, or confession—Memory is at the core. It is the conscious and reflective work of reconciling and *integrating* into our lives those elements from our past that are unfinished business.

Personally, we practice Memory in a number of ways. We may not have access to a confessor or a therapist (although if we do, we might want to consider them), but we do have ways of listening to our memories. For example, we always have access to prayer, to contemplation, and to ritual, practices that enable us to hear our memories and incorporate the unassimilated ones into our lives. We also have access to friends who will be there when we need them to help us in Remembering.

In *Prayer*, for example, we can set aside specific times where, having Centered ourselves and placed ourselves in the presence of the God who Cares, we gently and tenderly integrate a memory, retelling its story, and as we do asking for help—but without anxiety, irritation, or hurry. Or, we can set aside time to be still and *Contemplate* a memory, sitting with it in stillness, staying with the feelings it draws up from within us, and allowing both the feelings and the memory to wash over us and rinse through us, even if they bring tears. *Community* can assist us in integrating our memories too, especially if they are almost too painful to touch—incest or rape or the sudden death of a beloved person—by providing group settings where such memories can be faced in the companionship and support of others. Those others are there to hold and strengthen us as we weep.

And *Ritual* in the ancient form of casting out demons—*Exorcism*—can be designed in order to cast out the poison which some memories can generate in our systems, feelings of hatred and self-loathing, or urges toward violence and vengeance, which keep our wounds open. Memory practiced in these ways has, at root, a spiritual dimension and a bias toward health.

However, a second integration of past and present which Memory makes possible is the power to integrate our traditions into ourselves. More specifically, Memory is the spiritual discipline through which we "memorialize" and "re-member" the *people* who have made us *us*; the traditions—of family, town, country, religion, profession—that have formed us. This is the reason we have holidays, one of which is called Memorial Day in the United States; why we have statues and memorial services in public, and birthday cakes, pictures, and photograph albums in our homes. Memory—the telling, repeating, and recording of "our" stories—enables us to be in touch with our corporate and communal past, to meet it, and to integrate it.

In African religion there is no future. Time is composed of past and present. The older I become, the more that meaning of time makes sense to me. For as I move through life, the dance of my own spirit directs me more and more—toward the women and men who are my ancestors but who do not reside in a place named "heaven." They reside, instead, as do my other memories, inside me; their bodies and bones are interred in the planet upon which I walk daily, and their lives are interred in the human being I am and continue to be.

Justice

In biblical religious tradition, the meaning of justice is not the legal understanding that dominates our society. Instead, Justice has other, fuller meanings. One is *fidelity to the demands of a relationship.* In the Bible, not only are people considered just: A road is considered just when it leads to the correct destination; a song is just when its notes are in harmony. Human beings are just when we realize our relatedness to one another, to the animals, and to the rest of creation. We are just in caring for and being faithful to the demands of these relationships, in cultivating and not destroying them. This leads to a related meaning of justice—*as our continuing struggle to share the gifts of God's good earth.* Here Justice includes *finding out what belongs to whom and giving it back.*

In other words, Justice is the integration of the good and the not-yet-wholly-good. This is not only because we rejoice in the goodness and gifts of the earth, and therefore see their lack as an absence of goodness, but also because total goodness cannot be ours personally if others of us are without the gifts that rightfully belong to them too. As women, this has particular meaning for us, because more often than not it is *we* who know what *injustice* means. It is we who are trying to care for children without enough resources or we who have been neglected and harmed by profit-oriented professions and organizations. It is we who, as we become aged, are assumed to be useless as well.

Spiritualities that are incomplete, that do not see integration as essential, will tend to separate prayer and justice. That is not the route for women today. The route is, instead, that suggested by the prophet Micah:

> What does the Lord
>   require of you
> but to do justice and to
>   love kindness
> and to walk humbly
>   with your God? (Mic. 6:8)

Now, as in the days of the prophet, if we are to walk with God, we cannot separate companionship with God from compassion and justice.

As we come to the close of the twentieth century, this has become abundantly clear. The average United States citizen is in the top 1 or 2 percent of world wealth, and we have the greatest percentage of the world's goods. In addition, we are moving toward a time where, in our own country, 100 percent of those needing public assistance will be women— mostly Black, Hispanic, and old women. Given these realities, and the extraordinary abundance and giftedness of the United States, we who are the gifted ones are called not to guilt, but to gratitude.

But once we have rejoiced and celebrated our gratitude, we are then called to that piece in the mosaic of our spirituality that is the sharing of those goods—that is, to justice. Fidelity to the demands of *our* relationship with everything else takes the form of struggling to share the gifts of God's good earth. It is not difficult to find ways of practicing this form of spirituality, and if we are women in need of justice, we can help those who are looking to do so find others. But steps are open to all of us, every day, and embodied in the following commandments:

> You shall hold the resources of God's good earth tenderly, and with a light touch.
>
> You shall never forget to be grateful for all you have.
>
> You shall remember you are a steward of the gifts of the earth; you did not make them.
>
> You will give thanks minute by minute for your food, your shelter, your clothes, and those of your children.
>
> You will give thanks minute by minute for your job, your health care, your pension.
>
> You will not turn your eyes from the suffering of others.
>
> You will believe, and you will teach your children to believe, there is enough to go around.
>
> You will believe, and you will teach your children to believe, we are never diminished by giving.

Do these things, say the scriptures of all religions, and you will live. Do these things, and you will also love. Do these things, and you will be *whole*. For fidelity to the demands of our relationships integrates our acceptance of goodness in our own lives with a not-yet-universal achievement of goodness. Here is the mystic's understanding, once more: Everything and everyone is related to everything and everyone else. Which means no one can be *herself* without doing the work of Justice.

Adoration: The Undersong of Every Discipline

Reading this chapter on Nourishing, a person might assume she was reading a list of nine exercises, each one following the other in sequence. But a better image would be of three interlocking circles. And at the center of each circle would be the discipline I name now: Adoration. Adoration is not the last in a series of ten. Instead it is, like the Divinity Itself, the beginning and the end, the top and the bottom, the inside and the outside, *as well as the center*, of all spirituality. Adoration makes spirituality possible.

For Adoration is the discipline that acknowledges we did not create ourselves and we are not in control of the universe. Adoration is the discipline that compels us to say in one form or another, "Although I do not know Your Name, I know You are there. I place myself before You and participate with you in the making of the world. I have received all that is good from You: earth, water, fire, air; life, health, intelligence; other people, myself. I am ready to fall on my knees in wonder and in awe. I *believe* You are dwelling at the Center of all things, and I give you thanks."

Because of this Presence of the Holy One—Thou—we live and move and have our being. Thou is the Center, and with Thou and in Thou and through Thou we are born, live our lives, and gradually approach death. We may name Thou differently; we may not name Thou at all. It may be very difficult to believe in Thou, but somehow it is even more difficult not to. The Jews of the camps found God guilty, and then went off to pray. And to the one who says, "I do not believe," a Jewish answer is "Pray to God about that."

But the point to make here is that without a Center things will fall apart; they will not hold. Without a Home Base, we cannot find our place and we cannot find our peace. And Adoration as a discipline is the one that says Thou is our Center, Thou is our place, and our peace. Adoration is the discipline that nourishes by teaching: To fall on your knees is incarnation of the possibility that we are meant to be happy. Not how, or when, or in what ways we can elude agonies, despair, and injustice, but *that* such a possibility exists.

With that kind of faith, we can then join artist Corita in believing all the rules will be fair and there will be wonderful surprises. Even more important, we can look the next generation in the eye and have faith that we are handing on to them a world worthy of cherishing and passing on a life worthy of living. Nourished by the strength that disciplined spirituality gives us, we can find ourselves poised and ready to move with firm steps into the next movement of the Spirit's Dance.

And so we enter the Step of Traditioning.

The Disciplines of Nourishing

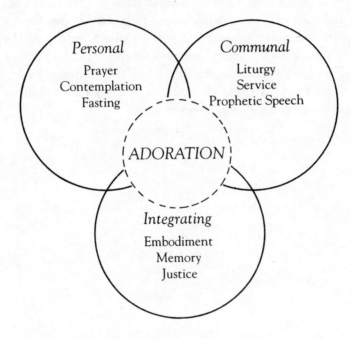

The Practice of Nourishing

Ideally, the seven practices of Nourishing are opportunities to engage in Nourishing as well as to deepen the Nourishing that already exists in your spirituality. Ideally, you should practice at least one of them every day, giving yourself a full complement of fifteen or twenty minutes (which may be divided into parts, or be expanded to twice daily, or in some cases not be applicable), even if you must rearrange your day. Done consistently, they will become rituals in your life; rituals that have their own rhythms and allow you to be nourished whenever and wherever you choose, as well as making Nourishing a permanent part of your spirituality, a permanent Step. The preliminary steps for each practice—or in some cases, the *preparation* for a practice that will be carried out later—are to:

> • Sit comfortably and easily, in a quiet place if possible, but on a bus or a train if that is necessary.

• Shut out any outside noise by attentiveness to your inner self.

• Close your eyes and become attuned to your breathing, to the rhythm and pace of your breath. Be sure to spend—at this Step—at least five minutes coming to awareness of your breathing. Inhale gently; exhale gently. Feel your body coming to a place of rest. For some practices, you will need to open your eyes after these first five minutes; for others the closing of your eyes is essential. You will discover for yourself for which ones closed—or open—eyes are appropriate.

Practice 1: Preparing a Diet for Our Spiritual Nourishment

Read the practice first. Then engage in the three preliminary steps. If it would be a help to you, engage in this practice with several other people. Sometimes a group can give us support to do something we really *want* to do but just can't seem to do alone.

At the beginning of this chapter, we read an assignment given to members of a class on spirituality. You are to do that assignment now, that is: Decide on a weekly personal discipline which includes at least *three* of the following:

- twenty minutes of prayer daily

- twenty minutes of contemplation daily

- one day of fasting (or one meal)

- twenty minutes of keeping a journal at least three times weekly

- one weekly meeting with other women to pray

- one weekly participation in a ritual with others

- at least three hours each week serving others

- one weekly participation in a human rights group

- walking, swimming, playing music at least an hour a day

- twenty minutes daily working through a past memory

- one evening a week working for justice

- twenty minutes daily being-with the Mystery at the Center

Promise yourself, or the group, to stay on this diet for at least one month.

Practice 2: The Prayer of Acts

Read the practice first. Then engage in the three preliminary steps.

The four purposes of prayer may be named: Adoration, Contrition (or sorrow), Thanksgiving, Supplication. This practice gives us opportunity to practice each of these.

Hold your life, as you did in Practice 6 of Awakening, as if it were a bouquet of flowers, or even a bundle of pick-up-sticks. Now let your life fall gently and naturally from your hands into four parts. These four will not necessarily be the same number of years. (For example, if you are thirty-six, they will probably not be nine years each in length.)

1. For the first part of your life, Adore the God who was God for you at that time in your life. Take time, do not hurry, and let your adoration be full and complete—and in whatever form feels most comfortable to you.

2. For the first part of your life, express Contrition or sorrow for those things you wish you had not done or left undone. If there is someone who was in your life at that time to whom you wish to express sorrow, or from whom you wish to ask forgiveness, do so now in your imagination. Again, take time, do not hurry, and let your expression of contrition be full and complete, taking whatever forms are most comfortable for you.

3. For the first part of your life, express Thanksgiving to God for the gifts of your life—parents, home, food, etc.—and especially for what may have been gifts uniquely yours.

4. For the first part of your life, offer Supplication, petition, or request for anything you might like to change from that part of your life—prayer, for example, for someone who was there for you, but for whom you never prayed; prayer asking for help for a part of the country where you grew up that is now in need, etc.

Now move on to the second, third, and fourth parts of your life, and repeat—taking as much time as you need—the prayers of adoration, contrition, thanksgiving, and supplication, as they feel right for each of the parts of your life as a whole.

Practice 3: Keeping a Journal

Read the practice first. Then engage in the three preliminary steps.

There are many ways to keep a journal. This is only one of them. The practice here depends on your preparing a notebook with ten sections: prayer, contemplation, fasting, liturgy, service, prophetic speech, embodiment, memory, justice, and adoration. During the twenty-minute period you set aside on either a daily or two- or three-times-weekly basis, record at least a sentence, a phrase, or a reflection about where you are in relation to each of these disciplines at this time in your spirituality. Give yourself a period of time, for example, three months, to examine your life with reference to these practices. Kept consistently over such a period of time, a journal can give you a picture of how your spirituality is being Nourished.

For example:

> *Prayer:* "Today, I prayed when . . ." or "Today, I prayed that . . ."

> *Contemplation:* "Today I had a moment of contemplation when . . ."

> *Fasting:* "Tomorrow, I will choose to fast from _____ for _____."

> *Liturgy:* "I realize I need rituals for _____."

> *Service:* "I was served today when _____ did _____."
> "I can do something similar tomorrow when _____."

> *Prophetic Speech:* "Today, I spoke out when _____. But I still need to speak out against _____."

> *Embodiment:* "I found myself feeling whole today when _____."

> *Memory:* "I need to integrate my memory of _____ even though it is still painful."

> *Justice:* "I have decided I will work regularly to end the injustice of _____ by doing _____."

> *Adoration:* "Today I found myself dwelling at the center of Mystery when _____. I will stop now at this moment and adore God present in that event."

Practice 4: Fasting

Read the practice first. Then engage in the three preliminary steps.

The preparatory part of this practice will be in the planning. The actual practice of fasting will take place during the day.

1. Choose one meal or one habit you would like to fast from during the day. Reflect on the meaning of this meal or practice as it presently exists in your life. (Suggested habits: shopping, watching television, staying home alone and feeling sorry for yourself, driving when you might walk, etc.)

2. Why have you decided to fast?

3. How do you expect to feel when the fast is over? (At the end of the day, or on the next day, reflect on your response and see if it is corroborated.)

4. Choose one person or group of people in the world in communion with whom you wish to join your fast (people imprisoned, an ailing friend or relative, a person who has asked your help . . .), or one person or group of people for whom you wish to offer your fast.

5. When the fast has concluded, take time to decide when you will practice fasting again.

6. End this reflection on your fasting by breathing silently for at least five minutes.

Practice 5: Holding a Dinner Party

This practice is based on the artwork of Judy Chicago, *The Dinner Party*. It is done with a group of women who wish to celebrate other women.

If the group is large, form into small groups of no more than five or six.

Each group is given a paper place mat and some crayons or paint materials (or more elaborate materials if that is possible).

Each group is then asked to choose one woman—well-known, little-known, or virtually unknown—whose Memory they wish to celebrate.

Each group is then given thirty to forty minutes to design a place mat for that woman.

At the end of the period, the place mats are put on tables that have already been set with glasses, napkins, and cutlery. The meal, real or imaginative, begins with the toasting of the women who are being remembered, and with a brief commentary on woman's life, for example:

> "We wish to toast Rosa Parks, a woman of courage who showed all women the meaning of human dignity by her refusal to obey an unjust, racist law, a woman who stands as a role model for women in the continuing work of justice," to which all respond: "To Rosa Parks!"

Practice 6: A Ritual of Responsibility

This is a practice engaged in together with a group. The intention of the practice is to create and engage in a ritual where the group (a) acknowledges past failure in taking responsibility, (b) promises present commitment to taking responsibility, and (c) confirms each person in the group in her decision to take responsibility.

Materials needed: a pitcher, a basin, two towels, water.

This ritual can be used by a group of women who come together regularly to pray, a group who work together in some service program, a group of women making a retreat together.

Opening Words:

"We come together to acknowledge both those times we have failed to take responsibility and the responsibility we now promise to take for ourselves, toward others in need, and for our world."

1. One woman is designated to fill the basin with water, and to act as leader, standing behind the basin which rests on a small table; two women, holding towels (or one woman, if the group is small), stand on either side of her.

2. Each woman walks to the center, and the leader dips her own hands in the water and then bathes the hands of the woman standing before her, as the second woman extends her hands over the basin.

3. The woman then moves either to the right or the left, and her hands are dried by the woman holding the towel.

4. When all the hands have been bathed, the leader asks the entire group to stand.

5. Each woman, in turn, then says her name, and the name of one person, activity, service, or word-to-be-spoken which she promises to do:

   Examples: "I, Selma, promise to take responsibility for volunteering one day at the shelter."

   "I, Dorothy, promise to take responsibility to complete the painting on which I am working."

"I, Laura, promise to take responsibility to call
on_____" (naming someone recently widowed).

To which the entire group responds, as each person speaks, "Selma, we
confirm you; Dorothy, we confirm you; Laura, we confirm you." When all
have finished, the group joins in applause and song.

Practice 7: Symbolizing Our Adoration

Read the practice first. Then engage in the three preliminary steps. The practice is meant to be done in communion with others.

Give each participant a paper with two columns, headed "Stops" and "Frees," and a line down the center.

Stops | Frees

1. Ask each person to choose a symbol, image, or metaphor expressing (a) what stops her from adoration, and (b) what frees her for adoration (ten minutes).

2. In a group of three, each person tells the other two which symbols she chose, *and nothing more*. She then listens to find out what the others saw in her symbols (ten minutes).

3. After ten minutes, the three engage in conversation about the symbols and try to confirm the person in her choice of freeing symbols.

4. After these ten minutes, move on to the next woman and repeat the exercise.

(The time can be shortened or extended for each person if necessary.)

Conclude by asking each person to tell the entire group the symbol that frees her for the practice of adoration. Then spend two or three moments in silent Adoration as a community.

6
Traditioning

A Pause for Centering

Let us begin by being still. Sit back in your spirit; do that by sitting back in your body. Breathe gently, slowly, and easily. This Sixth Step is Tradition-ing, handing on and handing over Spirituality to others. Let your own reflections on how spirituality has been handed on—traditioned—to you emerge from your inner self. Take time, do not hurry, and try to spend at least a few moments with each question. Do the same with each of your responses.

Is spirituality something that makes you feel comfortable?

Has it always been that way?

Have you ever felt that the spirituality you were offered or taught needed something more in order to fit you as a woman?

Were there older women who assisted you, as a child, to develop a spiritual life? If so, can you remember what they did?

Do you find yourself doing some of those things, now, with the next generation?

Are there women in your adult life who model spirituality for you; women you would like to imitate; women about whom you say, "I want to be like her when I grow up"? If so, can you pinpoint what about them or their lives is a lure for you?

Are there men in your life now how also model spirituality for you, men you would like to imitate? If so, what about their spirituality appeals to you? Is it something in yourself they mirror?

Do women younger than you, or girls, look to you for help in their lives?

Do they look to you for help in their inner lives? Their spiritual lives?

If a woman or a girl came to you and asked you for help in developing her spirituality, what would you tell her? How would you help her?

If you are the mother of daughters, how are you introducing them to spirituality? Are you? If you are the mother of sons, are you doing—or not doing—the same things?

Is there anything about spirituality you would like to share with the men in your life, things you see missing in their lives? If so, where might you start?

———————

Pulsing through the Sixth Step, *Traditioning*, is the music of an ancient religious song. We can find the song as far back as Plato; we can find it in the mysticism of Hildegard and Mechtild. We can find it in our own century in the art of Georgia O'Keeffe and in the writings of Etty Hillesum. The song is one that hymns in continuing rhythm, "The Good overflows itself, the Good overflows itself": *Bonum sui diffusivum est*, "the Good is that which, by its very nature, *has* to be diffused and shared." Just as light spreads silently into a waiting day, whatever is good in life tends naturally to overflow to others. Helping to make this happen, an essential part of the human vocation, is centered at this step. Our focus here is handing on Spirituality and the good we have learned to dance in our own lives to the next generation.

As this new step begins, the nature of the dance shifts to movement executed in partnership. Spirituality is recognized here as far too *good* a reality for only one person. For once a woman learns to dance spirituality, she cannot keep it to herself. If she wishes to possess a healthy and complete spirituality, she must hand on the treasure of spirituality to the next generation. This is the danceprint of *Traditioning*.

others, the realization that we have been traditioners comes accidentally, when a person names something we've done or said that changed her perception. For example, I remember talking positively in class one day about how little children's walking is a natural dance, rather than movement in learned, straight lines. A thirty-year-old woman came up to me in tears at the end of class. She said that she had been severely scolded as a child for dancing up the aisle during her First Communion. That day, twenty-four years later, was the first time someone had confirmed her childhood intuition that that was the right thing to do. And although the roles are many, Traditioning always demands at least these: *loving, teaching, mentoring,* and *modeling.*

About Loving

If the good is that which diffuses *itself,* the lover is the person who diffuses *Herself* and goes out to care for and to cherish. One of the most revered Names for the Divinity is Love—or *Caritas*—the ancient text reading simply, "God *is* love." What the text does not add, however, is that human beings are *also* love, and every time we express love for someone else, we are born a bit more into the divine image.

In Maya Angelou's poignant memoir of growing up in Stamps, Arkansas, entitled *I Know Why the Caged Bird Sings,* we read many descriptions of love on the part of adults for children—especially the love of older people such as her grandmother. One of the most memorable of Angelou's descriptions tells how the gift of reading was lovingly traditioned to her by Mrs. Bertha Flowers, the aristocrat of Black Stamps, and how through that first gift, reading, she was also given back her *voice.*

As a little girl, the child Maya had been raped. Soon after, the man who raped her was killed. Believing it was her words and her voice that had caused his death, and fearful that her speech could do further harm, the child stopped speaking. But Mrs. Flowers did not ask her to speak. She did, however, invite her into her home to have cookies and lemonade, honoring her silence during the visit. The first time she arrived at Mrs. Flowers's home, the older woman took down *A Tale of Two Cities* from the bookcase. "It was the best of times and the worst of times . . ." she read aloud, with grace and gravity. Angelou says that listening to that voice was like listening to singing; the beauty of the reading was that great. Indeed its power was such, and the love of the older woman so much at the

In psychological lore, a term related to Traditioning is "generativity." Popularized by Erik Erikson, generativity has to do with concern for guiding the next generation. Generativity assumes that our human lives are unfinished and wanting if we move through the cycle of birth to death without going beyond ourselves. We *need* to do things that improve the condition of children born and unborn, and as adults, we need to be needed. However, for us considering the spiritual dimensions of women's lives, a more fitting as well as historically religious term is *Traditioning*. The first time I discussed this with a group, a woman named Christina said, "Maria, I like the word; it *feels* like me as a woman." My hunch is it felt like that for her, as it does for many others, because it carries within it the interplay of both giving *and* receiving. We tradition to others and we are traditioned *by* others.

Mistakenly, *Tradition* is often thought of as words, rules, or doctrines handed on or handed over. But in a strange paradox this is not actually its meaning. For no such *thing* as "tradition" exists to be handed over. Rather, *it is the action of handing on and handing over that is the tradition.* Tradition is the process by which humans communicate *ways* of knowing, *ways* of being, and *ways* of doing from one generation to the next. Tradition is the handing on of *life* and of *living*, as found in exquisite description in the opening song, "Tradition," from *Fiddler on the Roof.* Tradition brings together past and present, just as Memory does. When we consider Spirituality as a *way* of *life* and *living* in the world—Traditio*ning* becomes the movements of handing on this life.

So, as we come into this step, we focus on (a) the *roles* the Traditioner dances, (b) the *qualities* of today's spirituality that *can* be handed on, and (c) the *family* as a basic context where women and men create Traditioning environments for their children.

Dancing the Traditioner's Roles

The step of Traditioning offers us many roles. Sometimes we learn these roles in our daily associations—families, temple, or church, and friendships Sometimes we learn them by observing how older women have traditioned spirituality to us. For some women, learning the step of traditioning planned and conscious. We intend and are even *trained* to tradition. Fo foundation of her attitude, that it caused the child to respond, to answer, and to receive. In the experience of being cherished for who she was and for who she might become, a gift—in this case reading—was traditioned. In Angelou's words, that in turn caused her to enter into the long tradition of Western literature, exchanging the bitter Southern wormwood that was her lot as a black child for a cup of mead with Beowulf or a hot cup of tea with Oliver Twist. And eventually it caused the child to reclaim her voice, and to speak once more, in tones heard today throughout the world whenever Angelou lectures or reads her poetry.

Bertha Flowers loved the child Maya into speech and into reading. But she did even more. For ultimately, she did what all great traditioners do: She traditioned and *gave* the child to herself. As Traditioners, we who arrive at this step in spirituality are to do the same, leading and loving children into Mystery and Spirituality, and in doing so, leading and loving them into themselves.

About Teaching

Our second role as Traditioners is to teach. This refers not only to those of us who are schoolteachers, although we are a critical group. It also refers to the teaching that continually goes on in any daily interchange of older people with younger, where we hand over ways of doing, being, and knowing. Adults are, of course, always teaching younger people informally through example and imitation—often they learn from us things we never intended. But there is also a more direct form of teaching where we *intend* to *show* and to *demonstrate*, to give directions, and create conditions for entering new worlds. At its best, teaching becomes setting "Existence Possibilities" before young people in such a way that we awaken thought, arouse interest, and provoke their desire. At the step of Traditioning, the Existence Possibility we offer is Spirituality.

With the youngest children, the best way of teaching is through doing things together: praying together, taking quiet time together, serving together, playing together. Just as we take time for daily meals, teeth cleaning, and washing, we take time to attend to spirituality daily—offering children its innumerable forms. Involvement in actual practices is a good beginning point, with time for reflection coming later on. But whenever the moments for reflection arrive, as in "Mommy, why are we doing this?" we take time to explain our dancing and how it helps us become whole, complete women.

The home, the synagogue or church, and the classroom are three of the most natural traditioning places, but there is no reason why the practicing and reflection upon spirituality can't be a part of neighborhood life, Girl Scouts, or other club activities. Any of these agencies might easily serve as sponsors for "Spirituality Days" or special weekend retreats for mothers and daughters.

Such practices ought to continue into adolescence, where young women are offered such forms of spirituality as poetry and prayers, stories and songs, as well as opportunities to create new poetry, prayers, stories, and songs of their own; where they are offered service projects to work with homeless, battered, and needy people. (Practices illustrating these are found at the end of this Step; others are offered at the end of Steps 4 and 5.)

Women whose teaching is in a religious setting, a Sunday school teacher, director of religious education, or minister, for example, have a natural vocation here. Not only can they offer such forms as part of their work, they can also be critical of other forms, especially those that are exclusively male, or that rely heavily on such images as *warriors* in battle, *soldiers* of God, *armies* engaged in warfare. For we are not bringing up our daughters or our sons to be war makers; we are traditioning them toward Peace.

However, the Traditioning of spirituality should not stop at the high school level. Women who are going on to college, or returning to school in later life, shouldn't have to search for courses in women's spirituality (or for that matter for courses in *spirituality*), which can be part of literature, history, art, political science, biology, psychology, sociology, and education, as well as religious studies. Currently, for example, four of the women in my spirituality course are nursing students. And Maura, a young woman I love dearly called me recently and added one more. Asking what I was teaching, and hearing my description of our course, she responded, "Hey, that's great! I'm doing that too—my management teacher always spends the first fifteen minutes helping us to meditate. It really changes the way we learn!"

But women who do not go to college should also have opportunities for deepening spirituality. No reason exists why businesses and corporations could not include teaching about spirituality as part of employee programs. If handball courts and dining rooms are offered to serve the body, quiet rooms and quiet times should be offered to serve the soul, and instruction in the many steps of Spirituality made a part of the business day. Japan has been doing that in one way or another for years. Such opportunities have a humanizing and healing impact on the frenzied pace of many business environments.

And finally, the teaching role of magazines for both girls and women should be taken into account—they are the major teaching vehicles and sources of continuing education for many of us. If every article on exterior beauty, diet, and shaping up could be balanced by one on interior beauty, nourishment, and calisthenics for the soul; if even one regular column on women's spirituality could be included in women's magazines, an instructed and spiritually mature cadre of women might be the result.

About Mentoring

The workplace and the job site are ideal places for the third Traditioner role, Mentoring. The name "Mentor" goes back to Greek mythology, where the first one to use it was the goddess Athena in her role as guide and counselor to the young Telemachus. Today, mentoring as a role has become prominent once again as women have reentered the work force, especially in executive roles. And even as we hear of women in competition on the job site, we hear even more of mentors for younger women in business, in medicine, and in academic life, where increasingly the guide for a women starting out is not, as in the past, a man, but another woman. Networks are flourishing throughout this country and abroad where women meet regularly to assist one another in learning the intricacies and politics of unfamiliar environments. And the role of mentor, understood here as an experienced person acting as guide and counselor to one who is generally a generation or two younger, is taking on critical importance.

A friend who teaches at a large Midwestern university recently told me a story about this new awareness of mentoring. In a course on psychological development, she regularly asks students to describe what is happening in several pictures. One picture portrays two women in lab coats. Her most recent class had three women out of a group of twenty whose immediate response when asked to interpret the picture was "One is mentor to the other." My friend says she sees this as a hopeful sign, and she happily contrasts it with a response she received only the year before from one of her male students. His comment: "They aren't doing anything."

Mentoring almost always includes some teaching, but its distinction lies in the relationship being one to one, with the additional elements of apprenticeship and overseeing of practices as components. The Mentor stands neither opposite, nor in front of, but *alongside*. One of the best-known mentors in recent storytelling about contemporary women's spirituality is Agnes Whistling Elk, the mentor of Lynn Andrews, whom we met at the first step. Agnes, the Native American wise woman, possesses critical knowledge of the way the earth works, and she teaches Lynn to know, from the inside, the relatedness of all things.

> Learning how to hunt and all that it entailed—such as classifying and recognizing the different qualities of game animals—was a full-time occupation. Agnes had an inexhaustible knowledge of wildlife and hunting . . . she had me tiptoe across the porch until I could show her that I could do it without making a sound. The task took me three days of painstaking effort to master, and by the end I knew every inch of the surface of the porch. I could finally step out from the edge and slip across in several different directions without a sound.

In terms of a more familiar and accessible mentoring of spirituality, a better-known and already-in-place role is found in Spiritual Direction. Here, as with counseling, a person meets regularly with a guide to explore her spiritual life. It is not unusual for me to learn, after teaching a spirituality course, that women in the course have gone on to work regularly with someone as spiritual director or mentor.

This is a formal arrangement, with its own rules and set of disciplines, and it may not be of interest to everyone. We need to exercise caution that the spirituality being pursued is designed for women, draws on women's lives, and is rooted in women's experience. But informally, if a woman is searching to deepen her spiritual life and meets another woman with whom she develops a resonating relationship as apprentice and learner—or, for that matter, a sensitive and sensitized man—the grace of that meeting should be acknowledged. She ought to trust her intuition that she is in the presence of someone who will enable her to claim a Tradition that is rightfully hers, and in doing so, enable her to become a Traditioner herself.

About Modeling

I once taught a woman who at the time was acting as graduate assistant to a famous male teacher of spirituality at an Ivy League university. Describing the experience to me, she spoke of it as largely positive, but then holding up her hands to form a circle said, "Yet we end each class with my saying to him, 'That was very good. But could you just shift"—here she moved her hands together clockwise—"about fifteen degrees? It is still off. It still doesn't quite "fit" my woman's life.' "

When I reflect on that conversation, I am persuaded how crucially we need other women to model spirituality for us—women with whom we can identify and who can serve as role models for us. This is equally true for the next generation of young women and for little girls. For, while many men are effective, understanding teachers, mentors, and lovers, it is nevertheless true that even the most sensitive men cannot "say" us from inside. And, although forgotten historical figures must be remembered, as we saw at the Second Step, we also need women in our lives today who are flesh and blood like ourselves. We need models who reflect ourselves to us.

Models exist for all of us in private and public life, and in fiction, drama, poetry, and the arts. Mothers are often, although not always, models for their daughters. But so too can be a mother's first cousin, one who never married, yet in no way exemplifies the cruelly stereotyped dried-up "spinster," being instead a vital, intelligent, humor-filled model. Or our mother's friends. Or our own friends. Or a co-worker who teaches us about the depths of living by the reverent way she treats everyone from the boss to a messenger.

Even more fundamentally, *every one of us*, at one time or another, is a model for what it is to be an adult, spiritual person. Whether aware of it or not, we are always asking one another, "What does your life tell me about my life?"—automatically observing one another to see how things are done. In a broader, more public sense, actresses like Colleen Dewhurst or Jessica Tandy are models for older women, being quintessential "women's women." Elizabeth Taylor is a model in her fight against pain-killing drugs. So too are writers like Alice Walker and Virginia Woolf and Audre Lorde, who "speak" our insides from *their* insides. Or wise artistic creators of people who mirror us back to hidden aspects of ourselves—women like Flannery O'Connor. Or television characters like Edith Bunker, Christine Cagney, and Mary Beth Lacey. All these women, either by their actions or their words, are models available to us daily. By taking careful notice of their ways of being in the world, we can learn to complete our own Traditioning, by waiting, watching, and drawing conclusions about the way we too want to *Be* in the world.

What Are the Qualities of a Traditioned Spirituality?

At the first Step of Awakening I cited accounts from women describing happenings in their lives that might be termed "religious"—experiences of Awakening. I want to return here to similar accounts, this time from three women remembering their *childhood*.

> As a small child one of my favorite festivals was Trinity Sunday. It seemed to me quiet and beautiful, and happening around midsummer became associated in my mind with green trees and flowers in bloom. It was "mysterious" and right, something far bigger than the words used in church about it which sounded to a small child nonsense. But Trinity wasn't nonsense, it was Holy, Holy, Holy, as we sang in the hymn, and even a very young child could join in a sort of "oneness" with all things bright and beautiful and worship this Something so great and lovely that it didn't matter at all that it was not understood. It just Was. (A woman, age sixty-four).

> Neither my mother nor father attempted to explain or describe God to me. God was indescribable as far as I was concerned, a Creator. But I am sure my parents increased my sense of God's omnipotence and mystery by their own awe and reserve in discussing the subject. (A woman, age twenty-three)

> My mother was an atheist, my father an agnostic. Religious ideas came through books, the colored fairy books, myths, legends of Greece and Rome, tales of Norsemen, etc. Religious feelings came from beautiful surroundings, the cycle of seasons, animal life cycles, looking at a speck of dust on a pond, and reflecting that inside oneself there was a center of quietness to be built up like this in expanding concentric circles. (A woman, age thirty-five)

In accounts such as these, we find a wealth of clues that can help us in Traditioning Spirituality. A *general* or all-inclusive clue is that spirituality is to be approached as an awesome and profound gift. But there are *specific* clues as well. These accounts are also reminders that to be traditioned at all, spirituality needs to be *appropriate, communal, recoverable* and *renewable, intelligent,* and *remedial* and *compensatory.*

Appropriate

The three women's accounts of childhood leave the impression that, as children, they were aware of Mystery even though they were not especially capable of talking about it. Still they had the capacity to appreciate its innumerable forms. Here, the clue for Traditioners is taking care that any spirituality we hand on to young people feels right; that it *fits* their experience. Most children will know that a center of quiet resides within themselves, but they will need help in reaching this center. When they do try to share with us their conviction that they are swimming in the heart of the Sun, it is not for us to correct, disagree, or point out that they are wrong.

For girls this obviously means continually affirming their female centers; it means strong and constant celebration of themselves in the way *they* are in the world. Being told that girls "can't" do something—whether it is becoming a physician, or getting dirty climbing trees, or leading synagogue or church services—can contribute to feelings of inadequacy and inferiority which inevitably will touch their spirituality. Ways must be found to celebrate femaleness, and rituals must be created for all the moments in girls' lives that are high points.

Among the ways for doing this, two stand out. The first is introducing a daughter to each of the practices of Nourishing: to prayer, ritual, justice, and adoration as symbols of the daily opportunities for spirituality. Each is an avenue she may travel in her move toward Mystery. Possibilities of practice are limited only by our own imagination (several more are found at the end of this chapter), and they can include such things as the child's giving thanks before a meal, cleaning and refreshing her body during a bath, and taking time to be quiet with her for "special" time during the day.

The second is to introduce her to many images of the Holy One, taking care that such images include all colors of skin. Along with being female, the Divinity *ought* to be traditioned as Black Mother, Oriental Holy Wisdom, Red Goddess. Otherwise, the images may not be *appropriate* and, even *appropriable*, more important. As adults too many women must still do the double work of relating to the Divinity solely with male images, translating and converting them as best they can into images with which they can identify. Although *told* we are in the image of the divinity, the images taught us are always male. Similarly, too many children of all colors, including white children, are offered images of an always white

God. In contrast, traditioning female imagery conveys to a girl that the Holy is like her, and she is like the Holy, at the same time it teaches her God is not reducible to any one image. God is, instead, her Mother as well as her Father, Bakerwoman as well as Shepherd, Homemaker as well as King. She is also Black, Brown, Yellow, Red. She is Rainbow too, the Eternal Bow in the Clouds.

One popular way to tradition female images is through telling stories of goddesses and mythic figures. Merlin Stone, for example, names the Celtic Goddess Cerridwen, who was the Goddess of Intelligence and Knowledge in the pre-Christian legends of Ireland, long before Patrick. She also introduces Lilith, the first wife of Adam, who refused to lie beneath him and cook his meals—who subsequently was unfairly named "Queen of the demons." And she reminds us that in the classical age of Greece, where the veneration of the Goddess as Artemis continued to thrive, women were extraordinarily free and independent. In our own time girls know something of what these goddesses represented, and how it feels to meet a larger-than-life figure *like yourself* whenever they pore over comics centering on the figure of Wonder Woman. Like their mothers and grandmothers before them, they appropriate her as one of *them*.

Communal

The Spirituality we Tradition to the next generation must also be a shared one, understood to be held commonly, a central theme at every one of the Steps. It must be based on the connectedness of all things and all people. The point here is to avoid conveying to our children that they have a "corner" on spirituality that others do not have or that their spirituality is only for themselves. Instead, if the Life we are handing over to them is to last, we must take pains to see that they understand it as related to earth and flowers and blossoming green, as well as to myths and legends and tales of the past, to stories of heroines and heroes.

At the same time, Communality demands that we teach our children their own participation in a People with a heritage and an abundance of riches, with roots and rootedness. This can be the people of a unique and particular tradition: Jewish, Christian, Muslim, Buddhist, Hindu—and the Traditioning of spirituality is helped immeasurably when a child knows herself to be part of a community that takes spirituality seriously. But an added dimension of her belonging lies in her recognizing she is a part of a *global* community and that she belongs to a People who

but also strong in the head. For human and spiritual wholeness, the heart and head must be integrated. Therefore a spirituality that is *intelligent* has the best chance of being traditioned for more than a season.

The young need to know—especially through teenage and young adult years, when their capacities for reflecting and criticizing are being developed and honed—that the reality being traditioned to them can capture as much of themselves as they are willing to invest. It can always be more than an appeal to emotion and feeling alone, if it challenges reason, intellect, and the capacity to analyze. It can be presented as a reality based on research, careful reading of ancient texts, scholarship, and intense study. A young woman who devotes herself to understanding it with all her heart and soul *and* mind will not be disappointed. She will find as much food for the journey as she needs in studying the work of women who have danced before her: women such as Simone Weil, Julian of Norwich, Evelyn Underwood, and Starhawk. Alerted to the work of these women, she is thus offered the possibility of developing support for her childhood's instinct concerning the presence of Something so great and lovely that it didn't matter if it was not completely understood. Reverence for her need to understand *now* will eventually bring her to that fullness of intelligence which is capable of understanding and going beyond understanding; and to a rediscovery of an enriched and deepened faith. An *intelligent* traditioning can bring her to the overflowing of intelligence known as Wisdom, even to Holy Wisdom Herself.

Remedial and Compensatory

Finally, a traditioned spirituality will, sadly, but at least for the time being, need to be remedial and compensatory. It will have to include the task of making up what has been lost and assume that women have as much to say concerning spirituality as do men. Traditioning will need to give special attention to finding forums where we speak together of the dynamics of Mystery, discover our own spirituality for ourselves, and recover what has been lost. One woman describes her own attempts at traditioning:

> I have spent the past year speaking to teenagers, and using
> people from the Scriptures as real folks that they can grab
> hold of and embrace. Every time I bring up Miriam, the sister
> of Moses, who saved his life, without whom the Israelites
> would have had to look for another to lead them out of
> slavery, they have no clue as to who she is.

Yes, *is*, not *was*. Miriam holds great lessons for us. What
does it mean to hold life as sacred? What does it mean
to use creative problem solving to deal with the impossible? What does it mean to look for what you have in
common with your greatest enemy to find life and salvation? Lessons we need. Lessons as great as the ones of
her brother.

Miriam is part of my blood, my life, as alive for me as
she was for Moses. I heard about Moses when I was five.
I found Miriam when I was thirty.

And finally, all the facets of Nourishing, whether prayer, service,
prophetic speech, or memory, will need to be practiced for a while out of
women's experience and changed as needed. Time is necessary for Dis-
Covering what is still lost, as well as for asking each other, "What is your
story?" "Where have you been hurt?" and "How do you find your God?"
And when we have these responses, we will be in a position to say, "This
is who we are, and this is our Spirituality." We will no longer need a
remedial step in Traditioning.

Where Traditioning Happens

What environments nurture the Traditioning of spirituality to the next
generation? Although the ideal setting is not confined to the family,
spirituality begins there, as the place where girls and boys grow into
adulthood in the company of mother or father or both. This is a first
reason why the family is *basic*. In addition, the family models qualities that
other institutions in society might copy and incorporate.

Even though the family continues to be the place where children
are nurtured, its *qualities* and qualifications in doing so tend to be down-
played, or worse, thought of as applicable only during childhood. In part,
this comes as a result of our contemporary passion for bureaucracy and *its*
characteristic qualities: division of labor, credentialing, objectivity—where
rules and regulations come before people, where precision and technical
skill are valued more than human affection. Even little children are being
encouraged to carry appointment books!

At their best, however, families are *not* mini-bureaucracies. Instead, they are the primary places for Traditioning to the young and for helping new generations understand their own capacities. For developing healthy spirituality, a different set of characteristics from the ones bureaucracy offers are needed, and these characteristics—a sense of rhythm, solitude, tolerance of failure, and commencement—exist primarily in the family environment.

A Sense of Rhythm

Most parents realize after a year or two of raising a child that human development does not happen on a set schedule. Instead, since each person possesses her or his own unique biological clock, a gradual unfolding takes place. Great variety exists from one child to the next. Still, each individual eventually embodies a general pattern which is more universal.

The first step in this pattern is physical—the baby showing extraordinary receptivity to physical stimuli and needing protection against excesses of noise, heat, and cold. At this time parents begin Traditioning spirituality by presenting zones of quiet, protective filters where holding and rocking provide peace. When speech arrives, a child will take hold of the rhythms of its own body and speech and then bring both—its physical capacities and its speaking capacities—to the great work of learning to play. This is the time when parents can help enormously through the kinds of rituals mentioned earlier: bedtime, mealtime, story time, and bath time, for example, where children need the stability of repetition.

Eventually, the child goes off to school and its playing becomes playing with ideas, numbers, and symbols—as well as playing with life. Now the child develops fascination with whatever exists, and if she is not impeded, her mind can roam over a wide field of interest. This is a time when she or he may love to memorize: poetry, prayers, parts in plays, lyrics of songs. And this is also a time when parents can love through listening, aware that another step in the rhythm is now emerging. Soon enough this fascination will give way to still another, as the child now becomes dogmatic, forceful, and often *right* about everything—fascinated with *its* own point of view. This can be a tough time in the family, but the good news is it will not last forever. Still for a while the young person will need to follow this path in order to get a sense of who she or he is and what she or he thinks.

Parents, however, should realize that their children are moving to another place during the course of these years. A sense of self begins to be strong enough to let them be *wrong* now and then. And being their own boss or having their own children modifies earlier notions, bringing them to a kind of conversion where they are willing to retrace steps, and even pick up elements they had not allowed in at earlier times.

The point is that the family is the place that either fosters or hampers this developing. If a sense of rhythm is present, the unfolding can go at its own pace; if it is not, the young person can be pushed too carelessly into a false mold. In fostering this rhythm, parents can be guided by two general principles: (1) The movement through life takes exactly that: a lifetime. And (2) there are times when the only thing to do is treat our child as we would a clam.

If we have ever tried to open clams that refuse to cooperate, we know the often fruitless effort expended. We search for a too sharp implement, or bang on the floor, or do violence to the shell. The alternative is simpler. Instead of probing, banging, or violating, put the clams outside in the noonday sun. The heat and the warmth will open them in their own time. A Traditioning family, living with a sense of rhythm, knows that life unfolds in similar circumstances. People *also* unfold in the warmth of the sun.

Solitude

"Loneliness," says writer May Sarton, "is the poverty of self; solitude is the richness of self." Solitude is very difficult for the poor; it is a luxury of the wealthy and of the middle class. Nonetheless, in Traditioning spirituality to all young people, an ideal worth striving toward is giving children pockets and spaces in their lives where they are free to enjoy solitude, to be by themselves, to take time for laziness, and to make the "siesta" the center of their spiritual lives. It is simply not true that an idle mind is the devil's workshop. Rather, as Sabbath reminds us, all of us need time for doing nothing.

Loneliness, isolation, and abandonment can be genuine terrors for a child, even more than they are for adults. Authentic solitude, on the other hand, provides the opportunity for children to be "watchers" or observers of life, getting the feel of its flow and rhythm. Talking about her Quaker childhood, Helen Flexner tells the story of how she learned to do this in her family.

> As a child I was told that grandfather spent an hour every
> morning and evening listening to God. So when I came

suddenly upon my grandfather one day seated motionless in his armchair with closed eyes, I knew he was not asleep. He was talking with God. I stopped short where I was and stood very still. Perhaps if I listened intently enough I might hear God's voice speaking to my grandfather. But the room remained quiet, not even the faintest whisper reached my ears. After a long time my grandfather opened his eyes, saw me and smiled at me gently. These moments of intense listening for God's voice in the room with my grandfather are among the most vivid memories of my early childhood.

We can only imagine what it might be like if all homes had designated "quiet places" where family members were encouraged to explore solitude. Perhaps families could arrange for one hour a week, or a half day a month, when they would agree to be quiet together to discover the depths of such riches. Schools might copy from the family in this; although most have faculty lounges, where teachers can withdraw and be refreshed during the day, too few have student lounges to provide similar retreat.

Solitude is not necessarily limited, however, to the absence of sound. Privacy can also take the form of a break from probing, judging, interrupting, and criticizing. Siblings often know one another's sorest spots and often engage in continual teasing when one of the members, often the youngest, would prefer being left alone. Allowing for the privacy of all family members can be the beginning of a prayerful attitude where Contemplation is Traditioned, even to a three-year-old. If families take seriously the suggestion to build on such privacy, they can contribute mightily to the Traditioning of spirituality in the lives of all family members, not only the children.

Tolerance of Failure

At the Step of Dwelling, we saw the power of Home as Dwelling place in the spiritual life. Poet Robert Frost wrote of home as "the place where when you have to go there, they have to take you in." So too with failure. Home is the place where it must be met; people live too closely in families, in the physical sense, to hide failure when it occurs. And the family's attitude to failure—in school, in games, in sports, in love—has a great influence on children's first encounters with brokenness, on their power to distinguish between trying and not succeeding.

One of the times Mystery is dis-covered is when a child experiences failing in others or in herself. This particular loss of innocence needs to happen if she is eventually to mature into complete adulthood. But spirituality is certainly Traditioned more fittingly when accompanied by the understanding that the divine Presence remains even in times of failure, and that spirituality includes a growing awareness of the presence of a shadow side of life. Acceptance of failure will therefore be essential to grasp the fullness of Present Mystery even in the difficult hours.

Families, especially the adult members of them, can make such acceptance a possibility for children if they themselves are able to accept failure. Often, the child is ready and able to do so, but because parents want to experience success through their children's lives rather than through their own, children are either not permitted to fail or are told that their pain, anger, and misery are not real. The Traditioning step of spirituality is the place for parents to become sensitive to this issue and teach the opposite response—that the family is a real world of real humans where many mistakes are made, where ambiguity is never far away, where lost tempers are admitted and found, and where failure is acknowledged and owned. In such settings, the Traditioning of forgiveness, joy, and spirituality may be buried for a while, but eventually it will flower from what seemed hard and bitter ground.

Commencement

Seeing the family as a place of commencement means it is a place that succeeds if its members can leave it. A family is a community that should serve as a model for all communities. To understand how difficult this can be, one need only ask a mother what it is like to send a child out to the first day of school; to ask a father how difficult it is to "give away" a daughter in marriage; or to watch a child choose a path different from the one the parent thinks best. It is important to raise children in the direction of *independence*, or better yet, of *interdependence*. And that means helping the young to live into their own decisions as they grow older, helping them discover their own unique gifts so they no longer need yours the way they did as children. When it comes to Traditioning in the direction of a full spirituality, it means sending them toward their own unique configuration of awakening, dis-covering, creating, dwelling, nourishing, traditioning, and transforming—even when that is difficult, or different from yours. In this, we dance Traditioning most artistically in our movements of letting go.

For the moment of genuine growing up begins when a young person realizes it is all right to leave home. A strength is given in such a time for young people to say of their family, "These people trust me. They aren't saying a lot, they aren't giving me orders, but they hear me and they care. They believe in my participating in the dance of the Spirit to which *I'm* called. They think I can do it."

The young realize, in other words, that we are not only Traditioning them a Spirituality; *we are Traditioning themselves to themselves.* The irony in the situation is well-known. Once the vision beyond the family, the going out, and the exodus are encouraged, it is possible to come back; indeed, it is the only way to assure return and fully claimed Tradition. The end of all exploring is arriving at the place from which we started and knowing it for the first time.

If, from the beginning, the environment has been one that traditioned "God is where you're going," that irony will not change. If the family environment has encouraged personal rhythm, has allowed for solitude, and has tolerated failure, then wherever life takes the now grown child, it will be in the Divinity's direction. It will be a dancing toward that fullness of Mystery that exists at the center of Desert, Garden, City, and Home. And there, even if the Handing Over has been imperfect as it is bound to be, children will find the inheritance Traditioned to them from the beginning; the inheritance of Holy, Holy, Holy; of Wisdom; of Wonderful Surprises; and of Goodness continually Overflowing.

The Practice of Traditioning

Although the seven practices of Traditioning are different in orientation from the practices of the first five Steps, they presuppose the same three preliminary steps required for the first five. They cannot substitute for the regular twenty-minute practice. However, they do represent a development beyond the practices of the previous chapters, where the major focus was on taking personal time.

The particular characteristic that changes in these practices is that they are done either in company *with* others, or they assume the person doing them is acting in a Traditioner role *toward* others: as Lover, Teacher, Mentor

Model—and sometimes as a composite of all four. Those practicing them should of course adapt or change where that is necessary. If the steps in the practice do not fit a person's experience, she should feel free to revise them.

Practice 1: A Scavenger Hunt for Women

The purpose of this exercise is to introduce young women (girls from eight to ten, teenage young women, young women in groups) to some of the forgotten female figures in myth and history who might reveal to them aspects of themselves. The hunt is in three parts: (1) naming the names, (2) holding a party, (3) reporting on experience. Ideally, the practice will take three weeks in all, with one day—afternoon or evening or both—for each part. However, more time may be needed for part 1, and the leader may want to suggest two or three weeks on the research.

Preparation: explain to the young people that they are going in search of forgotten or lost women. These women live in stories, inside people's imaginations, in mythology, in dreams. They can choose to go looking for the women alone or in twos and threes. But in part 1 of the scavenger hunt, they will be doing research. When they have found out everything they can about each of the people, they will move on to part 2, where they will come to a party dressed as that person and spend the entire party pretending they are that person—they must be in character the whole time. In part 3, they will meet to debrief, to assess, and to talk about the experience.

Part 1: Prepare a list of names, to be chosen from a glass bowl or a hat, which includes the following:

Susan B. Anthony	Hagar	Medea
Aphrodite	Hera	Miriam
Artemis	Hestia	Nefertiti
Astarte	Hildegard	Flannery O'Connor
Cerridwen	Inanna	Penelope
Demeter	Isis	Persephone
Devi	Judith	Phoebe
Dorcas	Kali	Rachel
Esther	Jane Lead	Rebecca
Eve	Leah	Shakti
Elizabeth Fry	Lilith	Sojourner Truth
Gaia	Queen Mab	Elizabeth Cady Stanton
Angelina Grimke	Mali	
Sarah Grimke	Margaret Mead	

Part 2: Together, prepare a party for an afternoon or evening, where the participants will come as their chosen person. Suggest they bring pot-

luck food, or gifts symbolic of that person—at least one food and one gift.

Part 3: Meet a week later to share what the young women have learned from their own research and acting, and from one another.

Practice 2: Teaching Meditation to Young Children

The purpose of this practice is twofold: (1) to give parents and teachers a simple process to hand on to children; and (2) to help children to enter their own inner centers of quiet. The practice has five parts: preparation, concentration, meditation, contemplation, closing moment. It is designed for children six to ten years old.

1. *Preparation*: Here the adult readies herself for what she is to do, along the lines we have set up in the first five chapters. Make sure the children are comfortable; if it is the first time, have a brief discussion about what they are going to do. A few breathing exercises can help.

2. *Concentration*: Choose an object such as a penny, a feather, a pebble, a picture. Give them time to concentrate on the object, to look at it, smell it, feel it, touch it.

3. *Meditation*: Having given them time to look at the object, the leader asks the children to put it aside and makes several comments. For example, a penny began in a mint, has been through many hands, has fallen on the ground and been picked up, has been in someone's pocket or purse. Talk for a few moments (not too long) about the object, and ask the children to think—to meditate—with you.

4. *Contemplation*: Direct the children to move into their own inner circle of quiet, their heartroom, their center. Tell them to sit quietly and try to remember that God or the Holy Mystery or their Mother God is with them. Tell them they are loved; they are pennies belonging to the Holy One. They are treasures. In other words, help them to identify with the object you have chosen. Help them to rest in attentive awareness toward the Mystery surrounding them, holding them, loving them.

5. *Closing moment*: After a brief time, tell the children they are

going to come out of their center of quiet. "Come out slowly
. . . take three breaths . . . open your eyes." Give the children
time to do this.

Practice 3: Finding Poetic Expression for Our Spirituality

The purpose of this practice is to put our meanings of spirituality into poetic form, again in a group context, although this is possible one-on-one between women and children. The poetic form used is the cinquain (a five-line stanza), which can prove helpful as a discussion starter, a way to explore a particular aspect of spirituality, or as a concluding or summary activity. Two forms of the cinquain are:

Form 1:

Directions:

Line 1: Give a one-word name, which is the subject of the stanza.
Line 2: Give two words to describe the first line.
Line 3: Follow this with three action words.
Line 4: Create a phrase descriptive of the subject.
Line 5: Summarize in one word.

Example:

Mentor
Solid anchor
Watching, guiding, pointing
Never out of touch
Mary

Form 2:

Here a cinquain is a five-line stanza in which the first line has two syllables, the second line has four, the third line has six, the fourth line has eight, and the fifth line ends the poem with two syllables.

Caution: In writing a cinquain, search for the precise word. Try not to choose a word just because it has a certain number of syllables, or to add a nonessential word just to fill the count. The challenge is authenticity.

Example:

(2 syllables) Stillness

(4 syllables) Cloak of music

(6 syllables) Rushing to crescendo

(8 syllables) Reminding me I must slow down

(2 syllables) Rest now

The beauty of cinquains is they can be created by anyone at any age—by the very young and the very old and all of those in the middle.

Practice 4: A Group Exploration of Spirituality As Traditioned

The purpose of this practice is to explore in a group the ways members of the group understand spirituality now, and how that is influenced by the way spirituality was traditioned to them. Ideally, the group should have time to prepare the responses to these questions, either before meeting or in the first part of the time together.

1. What words or phrases do you associate with the term "spirituality"? Can you remember the first time the word began to have meaning for you?

2. What feelings do you have, or do you associate with spirituality?

3. Complete: For me, spirituality is _____
   _____
   _____.

4. What is an experience you had in childhood you would consider part of your own spirituality? Are there any people you associate with this experience?

5. What is an experience you had in your teenage years you would consider part of your own spirituality? Are there any people you associate with this experience?

6. What is an experience you have had during the past week that you would consider part of your own spirituality? Are there any people you associate with this experience?

7. If you could choose one woman (real or fictitious) who taught you spirituality, who would it be?

8. If you could choose one woman (real or fictitious) who mentored spirituality to you—or whom you would wish as a mentor—who would it be?

9. If you could choose one woman (real or fictitious) who models/modeled spirituality to you, who would it be?

10. What aspect of spirituality do you most want to hand on and hand over to the next generation of girls and young women?

Practice 5: A Group Inventory of Images of God

This practice has as its purpose a conversation among several women around their images of God. Each person takes fifteen or twenty minutes to respond to the following questions (or if she is part of an ongoing group exploring spirituality, prepares her responses at home). After taking time to do this, she then talks with others about her responses. The result can be a person being in touch with the many ways Traditioning has gone on, not only in her own life, but in the lives of others. There are eight questions.

1. What were some of your images of God in childhood?

2. What images of God that you have met in this book have spoken to you? Which ones have unsettled or disturbed you? Can you say why you answer as you do?

3. What are some of the images you personally find expressive of what God is like for you?

4. Do you ever encourage your children, or younger people you may know, to explore and create new images of God? Why or why not?

5. If and when you pray, where—in what direction—is God? (Up, down, inside, outside, does not apply.)

6. Do you believe God can also be called Goddess? Why or why not?

7. Do you believe God can be found in nonhuman images: a great tree, a river, a song, a rock, a hen, a homemaker, a baker-woman?

8. Do you ever pray without images? Do you think that is possible?

Practice 6: A Retreat for Mothers and Daughters

A retreat is an opportunity to go apart and rest awhile. Retreats may be one day in length, one afternoon, one weekend, one week—even as long as a month. For those who have never been part of a retreat, a one-day retreat might be the best to start with. Preparation is needed beforehand, however, and a schedule should be drawn up, even if we expect to be alone. The following is a sample schedule for a mother-daughter retreat. Ideally, the retreat is held at a retreat house, or house of prayer, away from interruptions such as doorbells and telephones. Often these places are run by religious orders of women, and at such places spiritual directors are available if desired. However, people can also plan their own use of time.

9:00 A.M. Arrival.

9:15 A.M. Introduction and Centering or Quiet time. (Choose one of the practices suggested earlier in this book.)

9:45 A.M. Introductions. These can be done by asking people to say why they have come, or by using one of the inventories of reflection offered throughout this book.

10:30 A.M. Small groups. Daughters in small groups of three to four; mothers in small groups of three to four. Let the topic be what they want for their own spirituality. Use an exercise such as practice 4 or 5 preceding this practice to help start discussion.

11:15 A.M. Break for tea, juice, coffee.

11:30 A.M. Return to large group; share the small-group experience.

12:00 P.M. Lunch. Decide beforehand whether you wish this to be in silence. If so, choose background music (not hymns, however; rather such women singers as Judy Collins or Judy Small, or groups such as Sweet Honey in the Rock).

12:30 P.M. Organized recreation—games. Walk outside.

1:00 P.M. Quiet time.

1:30 P.M. Mother-daughter dyads. (See practice 7 following this practice.)

2:30 P.M.   Return to large group; share the insights and
              discoveries from the dyads.

3:15 P.M.   Ritual of Celebration. (See practices 5 and 6
              in chapter 5 for possible rituals that could be
              adapted, or design your own. This can easily be
              prepared beforehand by a committee.)

4:00 P.M.   Departure.

Practice 7: A Conversation in Dyads for Mothers and Daughters

A dyad is a two-person unit. This exercise is for mothers and daughters, but it can be adapted for other pairs of partners. And, although it is intended for use during a retreat setting, it can also be used as an exercise on its own anywhere.

Directions:

1. Reflect on the statements in the exercise* and then complete each one (suggested time: fifteen minutes).
2. Exchange papers with your partner and privately read the answers (suggested time: five minutes).
3. Take turns listening to each other's reactions to what you have read (ten minutes for each person).
4. Finally, freely share your responses with each other (suggested time: twenty minutes).

     1. I think my strong points are . . .

     2. I think your strong points are . . .

     3. I think my weak points are . . .

     4. I think your weak points are . . .

     5. One of my greatest fears is . . .

     6. I think one of your greatest fears is . . .

     7. I think one of the best things I have done for you is . . .

     8. I think one of the best things you have done for me is . . .

     9. I think one of my greatest achievements was . . .

     10. I think one of your greatest achievements was . . .

     11. I think one of the hard things about being your mother (daughter) is . . .

12. I think one of the best things about being your mother (daughter) is . . .

7

Transforming

THE SEVENTH STEP

A Pause for Centering

Let us begin by being still. Sit back in your spirit; do that by sitting back in your body. This Seventh Step is Transforming, not only our personal Transforming, but the Transforming of our world. The step is a culminating one, and earlier steps have been leading to it. The step is a birthing one itself leading to a new vision. But the step is an integrating, too, of all that has gone before. As you reflect, take time. Don't hurry. And try to spend at least a few moments with each question. Do the same with each of your responses.

Where were you ten years ago?

Who were you ten years ago?

As you reflect on the last ten years of your life, can you pinpoint where changes, or transformations, have come? Can you pinpoint why and how they've come?

Have there been silent parts of yourself you've begun to hear over these years? Have you begun to hear silent places in the world beyond yourself? If so, what are you hearing, and why do you think you are hearing it?

Have any of these discoveries of silence led you to raise new questions about yourself or your world? If so, what are some of the questions?

As you've listened to your own life, have you recognized any experiences you need to mourn for or grieve over? Are there memories or experiences of which you say, "I have to let go of that," or "I've never really allowed myself to grieve over that"? Do you resist mourning or have you made it a friend?

Where in your life do you find you've made new connections or formed new relations? Where in your life have you created bonds with other women? Where and how are you bonded with men?

In what ways are you bonded with the earth?

How do these bondings—or connections—contribute to your personal Transforming?

Have you ever had the experience of feeling you had given birth, although not in a physical way? To someone else—perhaps by being mentor or lover or model or teacher—or to a new relation with the world?

Have you ever had the transforming experience of giving physical birth to a baby? If so, can you name—at least for yourself—the effect giving birth had on your spirituality?

Have you ever had the experience of feeling you had given birth to yourself? If you did, was it an experience of Transformation?

In both the Hebrew Bible and the Christian New Testament, many stories are told of healing and new life for those who have given up hope. A prophet speaks, a stranger appears, a messenger from God arrives bringing extraordinary news. And miraculously, the blind begin to see, the lame to walk; lepers are cleansed, the deaf hear, the dead are raised up. These are descriptions of Transformation.

Often, these stories have to do with a birth. A woman discovers she is pregnant, and she sings a song of the soul, a canticle, as Sara did, as Hannah did, as Mary did. Sometimes, like Hannah's and Mary's, the songs get recorded. The Gospel of Luke, for example, tells us that when Mary discovered her pregnancy, she sang her song of new life to her cousin Elizabeth, telling the older woman who was her spirit's confidante, "My soul is big with God. And it makes me feel as if from now on, I shall have no endings. What is happening to me is happening everywhere: the mighty are falling; and the humble ones, the little people, are beginning to be lifted up."

It would be a serious mistake for anyone hearing such stories to think they were only about events long ago. For the Bible is there to tell us not only of them but of us. It has lasted all these centuries because its stories are about real human beings. If we search, we can find our stories in theirs.

We can find ourselves in the women who suffer terribly: Hagar, the other woman in Abraham's life, thrown out into the desert with her child, both of them unwanted. The daughter of Jephthah, killed by her father as a sacrifice, unlike that other better-known child, Isaac, who was saved at the last moment. Tamar, the gentle, innocent teenager cruelly raped by her own brother Amnon, both of them children of David the King.

But we can also find ourselves in the women who rejoice in coming through suffering: Naomi and Ruth, mother-in-law and daughter-in-law, who became each other's closest friend; Miriam, the sister of Moses, who helped lead her people from slavery and is the first recorded *dancer* in the Bible; Esther and Vashti, both standing up courageously to powerful men; Mary Magdalene, who knew what it was to love greatly and who wept her way into grace.

Finding ourselves; renewing ourselves. And realizing that because we have faced brokenness and come through it dancing and rejoicing, *we* are today's prophets. *We* are today's messengers bringing good news to the world. Transforming is the step where we recognize that the past is alive in the present. Transforming is the Step where we gather up the richness of previous centuries and previous steps and offer that richness to the world.

Transforming. We dance now into the great discovery that in giving birth to our Spirituality, we are giving birth to ourselves. And as we are reborn into self-possession and self-understanding, the power of that rebirth spreads out and spirals forth. Renewal in our own lives has the ripple effect of renewing the face of the earth.

In this chapter, we live into the rhythms of this renewal and we dance our finale—the five movements in the Transforming process. As we dance into the movement, each one enters us in return. And we find we are not so much dancers who *do* the dance as dancers who *become* the dance. The rhythm takes us from *Listening* to *Questioning* to a pause for *Mourning*. From there we dance on to *Bonding* and finally into *Birthing*.

This is a set of movements made by millions of women throughout the centuries. But now the turn is ours; the place is here and we are ready to become the dance.

Listening

At several earlier steps, we explored the crucial place listening has in the spiritual life: In *Dis-Covering*, it led to responding; in *Creating*, it prepared for Engagement; in *Nourishing*, it nurtured through prayer and contemplation. The Listening we gather into ourselves now draws on these previous listenings. Here, however, as the entrance into Transforming, listening takes the particular turn of listening not to what is said, but to what is *not* said. It is a listening to all the unheard voices—it is *a listening to Silence*.

Silence. It would be difficult to find a more pervasive theme in the lives of contemporary women than the theme of silence, with its accompanying task of finding a voice. Walk into any bookstore, and the titles of the books about women's lives are striking. Tillie Olsen reflects on the lives of women who might have been creative artists but had their speaking cut off by duty and custom. She calls her work *Silences*. The poet Adrienne Rich, challenging women to break from the passivity that still threatens us today, writes of our situation as one "Of Lies, Secrets and Silences." Nancy Falk and Rita Gross call the religious lives of non-Western women "Unspoken Worlds." Jane Martin names the educational vocation for women today "Reclaiming a Conversation." Alicia Ostriker studies the emergence of women's poetry in America as an experience of "Stealing the Language."

But we need not go as far as the bookstore to listen to the silences. All we need do is listen in on conversations where we women are describing our lives to one another. Note how common it is for all of us to use phrases like "speaking up," "speaking out," "being silenced," "not being heard," "feeling deaf and dumb," and "not saying what we really mean." And the point is that when we do that for any length of time, we eventually find that the listening fosters a transforming moment of hearing what is not said. A letter smuggled out of a Philippine prison before Marcos fell was composed of a single sentence that sums this up: "If you really want to hear what we are saying, listen to what we are not allowed to say."

Listen to what women have been forbidden to say. The listening of our own era has been particularly healing here and has already contributed to Transforming. We possess a much greater awareness of the centuries of silence surrounding women. These silences range, for example, from the burning of European so-called witches, who were often older women, to the practice of Hindu suttee, where widows were burned with their husbands upon the funeral pyre. "The widow walked into the fire proudly and by deliberate choice. This was her way of showing the depth of her affection, her devotion, her fidelity" reads one incredible interpretation. They include the silences surrounding Chinese foot binding, heightened in its pain since women were the ones who did the binding. We now realize what a cruel comment it is to refer to someone as a "China doll," since this phrase meant a woman was carried because she had been intentionally crippled. We learn of the still-continuing practices of African genital mutilation and the still-continuing practice of unnecessary mastectomies and hysterectomies in U.S. gynecological practice. We are forced to listen to the unheard voices of the women who suffer these outrages, and who—because they are our sisters—are sedimented in the lives of all of us.

Careful listening helps us notice the connections between such practices and certain forms of spirituality. The witch burnings, for example, were sanctioned by the church; the widow burnings were affirmed in Hinduism; the mutilations have gone largely uncontested by religious groups at home and abroad. And we realize a connection exists between this history and the absence of a genuine spirituality created by and for women. We see the implications of the absence of women from roles where we might listen as advocates for one another. We recognize the need to work both on our own and *in mutuality* with men to create a spirituality that affirms the full humanity of women. Advocacy, mutuality, and affirming women's humanity are ways to eliminate such suffering in the future.

The sobering effect of such Listening naturally provokes a further demand to explore the listening that still needs to be done, and eventually to find out how to break the silence that destroys in order to give birth to the transforming silence of mysticism and the transforming speech of prophecy. It recalls us into another listening we may not yet have done: listening to the silences within *ourselves*. Genuine spirituality teaches a receptivity to rather than a denial of ourselves. Genuine spirituality teaches that we must love one another *as we love ourselves.* Genuine spirituality teaches that listening to ourselves and everything else is critical to Transforming.

Whenever I raise this issue with a group of women studying spirituality, I have learned to expect two responses. The *first* is the honest complaints that we haven't the time to listen to ourselves, or the house is too noisy, or the demands of our job or children, or whatever, make that impossible. The *second* is the remembering, by someone in the group, of how her mother or her aunt or her grandmother used to create space to listen to herself. "My grandmother used to put her apron up over her head," said one woman, "and we all knew that she was taking quiet time." "My mother did something like that," says another, "but she did it by sitting in one special chair in the kitchen. When she did that, all of us knew she was taking time to listen."

The necessary partner in genuine listening to our own heart's song is, of course, listening to each other and believing that all our voices are worth hearing. This is critical listening, for even today too many women have been taught, "Don't speak." Too many still believe that unless they keep still they will be beaten, either physically or psychologically, and unless they are seen but not heard, at work and at home, their economic security will be taken away. Still other women have been told since childhood their voices were worthless; either explicitly or implicitly their words have been dismissed. In effect, this has meant that over the course of an entire lifetime some women have never listened to themselves. Or they have listened to only the parts of themselves society said were acceptable. In working with women becoming aware of these personal silences and beginning to be aware of the sound of their own voices, I have regularly offered the following passage from a Margaret Atwood novel. In listening to it, many express a shock of recognition:

> This above all to refuse to be a victim. Unless I can do that,
> I can do nothing. I have to recant, give up the old belief that
> I am powerless and because of it nothing I can do will ever
> hurt anyone. A lie which was always more disastrous than
> the truth would have been. The word games, the winning
> and losing games are finished; at the moment there are no
> others but they will have to be invented, withdrawing is no
> longer possible and the alternative is death.

Confronting our own silences, and listening to ourselves, eventually moves us toward listening to other, previously unheard silences. To the silences in many men who have had to quiet the expressive parts of themselves if they wished to be accepted by other males. To the silences of children, too often "shushed" as having nothing to contribute. To the silences of Earth, in its land and air and water, so often in pain where we have abused it, as well as to the faulty systems, structures, and customs that reinforce such troubling silence.

As our Listening deepens, we inevitably touch the Center of all stillness. In the midst of all the silences, we become able to hear the quiet Presence of the One who loves us, cherishes us, needs us. And we move into the silent attentive Presence listening to us even before we have found the words that beg, "Don't question me, don't talk to me, don't touch me. Stay with me." We meet the Holy Mystery whose listening to *us* is the primordial power, hearing us into speech.

Questioning

The movement emerging out of listening is finding a voice. But at Transforming, the voice we discover is one that takes a special form: It is a voice that asks questions. Genuine listening gives birth to genuine hearing, and when we begin to hear, we also begin to ask, "Why is this so?" "Why has this happened?" "Who decided it would be this way?" And, when it comes as a movement in Transforming, "How might this be changed?" "Is there something I can do?" But we also begin to realize ours are not the only questions. While we are questioning, we are also *being* questioned.

Religious traditions have had an ambiguous relationship to questioning. On one hand, questioning has been viewed as troublesome, even revolutionary and rebellious. Dissent has been quashed. Those who in later times have become venerated as holy have in their own times often been cast out or martyred because they took to task established ways of doing things, or challenged existing systems as *not* being of God. Sojourner Truth, eventually freed from horrifying slavery, was one; so too was Anne Hutchinson, publicly banished from the seventeenth-century church in Boston. But on the other hand, religious traditions have also preserved the practice of questioning, from the ritual Passover queries in Judaism to the theology of revelation in Christianity, which believes in a continuing asking of the question, "Is there any word from the Sacred for me, for us, *now*—in our own time and place?" Such questioning is the way the traditions allow themselves to be challenged and changed. And, at their chastened *best*, religious traditions have taught that human beings *are ourselves questions*—put by God. *We* are questions put to one another.

Among the most persistent and demanding questions of this human kind are the silent people of our earth, especially silent women. As we dance into this seventh step, we not only *listen* to the silences they are, we ask questions about it. The steps that have preceded this one have brought us to the place where our attention moves beyond our own private lives. And so we ask not only, "What are the silences saying?" but even more enlighteningly, "What are those who are silent *doing,* and what has caused their lives to be shaped in this way?"

The answer is not difficult to come by. The silent and *the unheard* of our world are usually found making the world's beds, cleaning the world's debris, wiping the world's noses, caring for the world's sick and aged, bringing up the world's babies, and cooking the world's food. In other words, they are doing the daily, human, caring work—feeding, clothing, sheltering, warming, healing—that makes the planet run. In awesome disproportion, they are also doing the world's suffering and the world's dying. And overwhelmingly, the silent are women, whose faces we know from the nightly news, but whose *lives* we recognize from the inside. The long sojourn every woman spends in the territory of the silent has taught her its geography and landscape.

Which brings us to an even deeper level of questioning: the question of our *community* with the silent women. Community has been a central theme at each step, but here at Transforming, it flowers fully. For if ours or anyone's spirituality is to stay alive, it must be global and universal; it must be a movement toward Communion with everyone and everything.

As we have already seen, the human vocation is to listen. But it is not only that, for as humans we are to listen, and then to respond. At this point in the movement, we are learning to ask questions, and we are learning we *are* questions. But at the profound and spiritual base of this movement, we dance into the realization that *we* are always being questioned, and that the questioning of this step is not only the questioning we do, but the questioning we receive, and our response-ability to it.

When Community is the question, the response it calls forth from us is the completion of a spirituality where we now begin to live the conviction that our dance of the spirit must not be between God and our individual selves. Instead, spirituality must be transformed into a dance of ending the separations between us, lessening the divisions, and moving toward a universal sisterhood-brotherhood where the voices of all people will be reverenced and heard, and the lives of all people will be cherished. If we are Listening and Questioning, we have already begun the movements in this direction.

But now, if we are willing to continue this work and take responsibility for it, we will inevitably push on to the work of Birthing. A work women have always done, Birthing will not refer this time to the birth of a child. It will refer instead to the birth of another kind of world. And it will mean agreeing to do whatever we can to *transform* the face of the present world.

Further, it will mean recognizing that if anyone suffers, no one can be completely happy; if anyone is dying, no one can be completely alive; if anyone is without the conditions for change, no one can be completely transformed. This will not, however, impel us immediately into movements of action. Instead it will cause us to pause and be still as we enter a place of sorrow. Listening and Questioning will bring us to the pause of Mourning.

Mourning

When full Transforming beckons, and Questioning takes root, the temptation often is to try our best to *do* something, as in "Don't just stand there, *do* something." As we found at the Step of Dwelling, when we faced our deserts, the temptation often is to take as our slogan, "It is better to light one candle than to curse the darkness."

The Step of Mourning stands as a sober corrective to this attitude, reminding us that if terrible things have occurred, a necessary move is the not-doing of Sabbath. We need to stop in order to pause and mourn the unheard voices and grieve for their suffering, past and present. We need to acknowledge our own complicity, our own responsibility. We need to admit, sorrowfully, that our *not* listening and our *not* questioning contribute to the circumstances that keep our world from being healed. Instead of calling out to God that we are there to help, we need to ask God to be present with us as we face the evils of division, human greed, helplessness, enforced silence inside ourselves as well as outside. Instead of singing the old spiritual, "Oh, Mary, don't you weep, don't you mourn," we need to weep; we need to mourn.

For if we are to entertain the notion that a Transforming spirituality means *listening* and *caring for* people who have been forgotten or dismissed, and if a Transforming spirituality is one that takes seriously and *incorporates* the silences of people who are called to be in community with one another, then many of our former practices and attitudes have to go.

Our listenings and our questionings call for a sea change. They call for a spirituality that results from the coming together of the perspectives and the experiences of all people—and of the planet Earth too. At this point in the dance of the spirit, they also call for a spirituality that includes entering the depths and dying.

But not dying into death. Rather, it calls forth a spirituality that is a dying into life. And the best movement I can offer for this in a spirituality worthy of a *community* of people with *a capacity for the universe* is Mourning: discarding what is no longer viable in order to turn toward re-forming and trans-forming Spirituality. For that to happen, something must be allowed to die—in this case, a too limited spirituality from the past, where perhaps we concentrated only on our individual selves—and we need time to grieve its passing. And so we ask, "What *is* Mourning?" and then "How do we enter it?"

In 1942, after the Cocoanut Grove Nightclub fire in Boston took the lives of 492 people, Erich Lindemann interviewed the survivors and gave us one of the first extended descriptions of mourning. He named six characteristics: somatic, or bodily, distress; intense preoccupation with the image of who/what was lost; guilt; a disconcerting lack of warmth; disorganized patterns of conduct; and the feeling you no longer fit.

In reflecting on the transforming of ourselves and our spirituality, I find a remarkable congruence between those characteristics and much that is happening to women today. For when we labor to give birth to a spirituality out of the fabric of our women's lives, the mourner's feelings of pain, not-fitting, and being cold can envelop us. We may feel ourselves not only preoccupied but obsessed with teachings and ways of knowing we realize are no longer ours. We may find ourselves feeling guilty because we are depending more on ourselves and other women than we are on men, especially clergymen. Someone may even tell us we are not acting "like ourselves," whereas at some deeper level we know we have never been *more* ourselves. And so if this should happen, knowing the signs of mourning can enlighten and sustain us.

Physician Elisabeth Kübler-Ross continued this research and elaborated five stages: denial, anger, bargaining, depression, acceptance. I think of my own denial after Awakening, denial of the silence I experienced because of my gender; my initial refusing to acknowledge that I had been silenced because I was a woman. I had been educated; I was among the small percentage of women teaching in graduate school in this country. I think of my dawning sense of profound loss when I began to realize the spirituality I had never received, and the women of great beauty and goodness whose stories, whose names, and whose ways of living had been left silent and unremembered because they weren't deemed important. I came to realize finally, that when old ways, old forms, and previously sufficient patterns of life are being let go, I needed, as we all need, time to grieve their passing.

And when it came time to acknowledge my anger, I realized that was part of mourning too, and that it was all right to be angry. I even came to know what the theologian Beverly Harrison names as the *power* of anger in the work of love; I came to realize the ancient adage that hope has two lovely daughters, *anger* and *courage—anger* so that what must not be will not be, and *courage* so that what should be will be. I even found myself, when considering the loss and silences surrounding women's lives, taking as a mantra the teaching, "Whoever is without anger, when there is cause for anger, sins." In other words, I dis-covered Mourning as part of Spirituality in a deeply personal sense.

At the same time, however, I found that mourning is not only personal; it is social and public too. I found that whole groups of people must go through mourning together in ways that lead to Transforming, whether the groups are parents of disabled children, workers with black lung disease, employees of a company that has suddenly gone out of business, bereaved companions of AIDS patients, or widows facing the future without a beloved partner. We must descend into hell, making the passage down into grief and darkness on our way to light.

Once we make such a passage and give ourselves permission to *feel* the passing of former ways of seeing, listening, and hearing, we discover in our lives a circumstance pushing us on to the next movement. Having danced the mourning process and given it and ourselves time, we notice that *our hands are free.* We are no longer clutching the past, holding on to a life that is over. Instead, finally, we have *let go.* And with our hands free, we can now lean into the movements that complete the Step of Transforming. In a company of partners, and no longer solitary, we can extend our hands and dance into the movement of Bonding.

Bonding

Few themes are as central to women today as Bonding—the coming together, joining, and networking of people in order to create something new. Along with Disbelief, Bonding is one of the two great powers of the weak. Bonding is not only the experience of *being* together, it is also the work of women actively *coming* together to design and shape a world for our daughters and sons in which the spirituality we Tradition to them will be based not on individual holiness, but on mutuality, connectedness, and relation.

Bonding. Study for a moment several examples of women bonding. First are songs. From "Bread and Roses," where led by Judy Collins we sing, "No more the drudge and idler, ten that toil where one reposes," asking for a common involvement in work; to Holly Near and Ronnie Gilbert singing, "We are young and old together, and we are singing, singing for our lives; we are gay and straight together, and we are singing, singing for our lives; we are rich and poor together, and we are singing, singing for our lives," to Cris Williamson singing, "Lean on me, I am your sister; believe on me, I am your friend," the theme of bonding is present.

Bonding. It's a part of women's history—the family of Pankhursts in England, Emmeline, Christabel, and Sylvia (not as one writer referred to them, "Richard Pankhurst's wife and daughters"); Sojourner Truth working with Sarah and Angelina Grimke; Elizabeth Cady Stanton and Susan B. Anthony—the theme of bonding is present.

Bonding. There are the novels of our girlhood, our young adulthood, and our mature years: the Bennett sisters of *Pride and Prejudice*; the Marches of Louisa May Alcott's *Little Women*, Marmee, Meg, Jo, Beth, and Amy; Liz and Eleanor and Isabel in Mary Gordon's *Final Payments*; Charlotte, Felicitas, Mary Rose, Muriel, Elizabeth, and Clare in *The Company of Women*; Shug and Celie in *The Color Purple*.

Bonding. Finally, there is religious history: Eve and Lilith, Ruth and Naomi, Mary and Elizabeth, and the great Hindu goddess Devi, embodying the theme of Bonding in her own self, worshipped as Kali, as Maya, and as Shakti—not a Holy Trinity, but a Sisterhood of divine persons. If we are justifiably angry that so little is made of this history and imagery, good. We should be. But we need to start learning from it now, for it illustrates for us, out of our own stories, our profound and gifted capacity for human relation. Bonding illuminates for us our capacity to be sisters not only in one communion and tradition, but throughout the world. And it brings us to the ways we might Tradition and actually *be* symbols of Bonding for generations yet to be born.

A first Bonding, which we have already reflected on, is with the forgotten part of ourselves. Since there are parts of ourselves that resist bonding, as well as parts of ourselves that reach out for it, a powerful exercise is to think of each of these parts of us as actual people and to personify them so they might have a conversation. Ask them to speak. Having such conversations—either by ourselves or with others—often helps people knit together separate aspects of themselves.

Such bonding can serve as a springboard for bonding with other women. If the women are present to us and we have both time and circumstance, we can set up actual rituals, as we saw at the fifth step. However, if the women are across the country or across the world or across the centuries in our past or futures, then the power of our imaginations must *make* them present through imagery and fantasy, recollection and re-membering.

The most difficult Bonding, however, yet perhaps the most necessary, is the one about which we have spoken very little in this book. And we have spoken of it little because, although it *is* so important, it is dependent on our going apart, resting awhile, and finding out by ourselves and on our own, who we are spiritually. I speak here of the Bonding that is only fully possible when we have taken possession of ourselves as women, and can bring complete, mature, human selves into complete, mature, human relations. I speak of our Bonding with men.

Bonding with men: with our husbands and sons, our fathers and grandfathers, our lovers and friends, our bosses and co-workers, our students and patients. With the men who love us and the men who frighten us. With the men who intimidate us and the men who bless us. With the men who after all are themselves only human. With human beings who are also searching for what it is to be whole, complete, and spiritually alive in a world where too many of them are also silenced. With the men who must go through their own Awakening, Dis-Covering, Creating, Dwelling, Nourishing, Traditioning, and Transforming so that we might finally dance together.

Women bonding within ourselves and with one another as sisters is a prerequisite for male-female bonding. For it is not possible for bonding between the sexes to occur if it is based on an ideal of male bonding, or brotherhood alone or on a spirituality drawn solely from the lives of men. It cannot happen unless we know ourselves to be partners and companions.

Brotherhood as an ideal has been with us in history and religious life for centuries and has often stood as a good ideal—in fact, better than many others. But because it has been based on images of male bonding alone, from Jonathan and David in the Bible to Butch Cassidy and the Sundance Kid in the movies, it has not mirrored the fullness of the human or been complete. It has not led to Transforming in the lives of women, because it has not included the ideals of Woman Bonding and Sisterhood.

Without our sense of ourselves as sisters—companions and not competitors—we cannot be transformed into a Bonded human community. Our history of difference, separation, unequal division of labor, economic dependence, physical abuse, oppression, and silence is too great. Our own completeness as human people is still very fragile, for some of us so fragile we are still mute. Is it only in this century we have begun to vote? To hold office? To go to college? To be physicians? To keep our own names? To be no longer seen as property? And these only in *some* countries of the world? Have we any idea how close we are to the *beginning*?

Still, we *are* at a beginning and the breakthrough not only of sisterhood, but of sisterhood *in partnership with brotherhood*. We are at the threshold of a new time where as sisters and brothers we might move together into genuine Transforming. Sister and Brother: This is a vocation open to all—and it is the Bonding of Sisterhood that leads to it.

Sisterhood: a rich, textured title of cooperation and interdependence, hallowed in orders of women—not just religious orders of nuns, but in Hadassah by Jewish women, as well as in the use of the term "sister" for each other in the black community. Sisterhood. It is a name we use for our Bonding with our planet as well—the Earth, which knows it is not only our Mother. The Earth which knows it is also and even more fundamentally our Sister.

Bonding, Sisterhood, and Brotherhood lead to a spirituality built on community, communion, and companionship. I offer the word "Companionship" as especially revealing here, in this next-to-the-last movement in the Step of Transforming, as meaning more than someone associating with, or living with, or dwelling with another, but in its etymological sense of meaning "with bread." For only when we bond together to break bread, and share bread, will we be true companions to one another. It is then that we shall be able to reach a final movement in Transforming rhythm. Emerging out of Bonding, we shall enter the labor and the ecstasy of Birthing.

Birthing

In chapter 5, in attending to the meaning of Contemplation, I spoke of my friend Ruth, seven months' pregnant. Her baby is born now, and she is home in Switzerland. But just after the birth of Simon David she wrote, "The experience of labor and birth is still very much in my mind. I have never been that present in my life. All my senses and feelings were focused on that miracle going on. There was no room for any other thought, past and future collapsed in that very moment. We still feel like celebrating and cannot be other than just full of awe toward this beautiful, new life. Slowly, very slowly, I find my way back to reality, or better, to the other side of reality. I am starting to feel a deeper responsibility toward the future; it is as if the future has become personalized in our child."

Not all of us are able to describe birthing as eloquently as Ruth does; nevertheless, she is right. Birthing, whenever it occurs, is miraculous and full of possibility. As Ina Gaskin tells us, "Pregnant and birthing mothers are elemental forces, in the same sense that gravity, thunderstorms, earthquakes and hurricanes are elemental forces." And this is true of the birthing that completes the Step of Transforming, the birthing that is the completion of the Dance of the Spirit. When it happens in us and to us, we know we are changed people. We know we are finally ourselves.

The theme of birth has only recently entered the mainstream of spirituality. In the past, the theme of death has been far more evident. Economist and philosopher Charlotte Perkins Gilman noted some of the differences between birth-based religions and death-based religions early in this century, differences that apply to spirituality as well. She suggested they came from two fundamentally different attitudes: one arising out of the crises of male experience, one out of the crises of female experience. She said that for man, historically as hunter and warrior, the pivotal experience is *death*, both as killer of animals and other humans and as one threatened by violent death himself. In contrast, she pointed out, the pivotal experience for woman is *birth*, and the basic concern is nurturing ongoing life.

Extending that to religious life, she concluded that to the death-based spirituality—or religion, as she named it—the main question was "What is going to happen to me after I am dead?" whereas a birth-based spirituality asks "What is to be done for the child who is born?"—the question sedimented in my friend Ruth's comments on birth.

Women today are indebted to Charlotte Perkins Gilman, as we are to all questioning women who have gone before us. Still, I believe we need to alter her perspective to get at the fullness of spirituality. There is no either-or between birth and death in life; both are givens. But there is a relation of balance between the two, and genuine spirituality must tilt that balance toward birth. Death, dying, and mourning are necessary passageways through which all human beings must travel—throughout life and after life—but hope and wisdom hold out Birthing as the outcome and culmination of that travel.

It is the women of our world who can contribute to the entire human community the firsthand accounts of precisely what is involved in birthing. And if we would admit that Birthing is central to spirituality, we could learn new ways of exploring the vast uncharted places within the human heart. We could realize that although Birthing is a process known *physically* to women, it can always be incorporated into the lives of men and children and nonmothering women as well, as a symbolic and metaphorical power.

A first learning we might draw from Birthing is the realization of Bonding as the essential condition preceding it. The physical manifestation of this in plant and animal life is obvious. The poetry surrounding human sexual intercourse is a reminder that this human intimacy is in the direction of something being born—either in the relation itself, or in the new life issuing from it. Birthing does not result unless we have been with another in a mutual self-donation. It does not happen unless we have bonded.

Birthing also teaches a different sense of time. The human preparation period for birth takes nine months and refuses to be hurried. For those of us trying to develop a life of spirituality, birthing teaches patience, presence, and resting in the moment. Birthing teaches the riches found in Waiting. Birthing teaches that even when we are Awakened and involved in serious exploration and Dis-Covering, the moments of Creating and Dwelling arrive in *their* time, not in ours. New life claims us when it is ready.

Birthing also takes place in hiddenness. Even with sophisticated technology giving us all kinds of information about the future of the fetus, the daily movement toward birthing happens in darkness and away from glare. Here, darkness is a good. One of the great learnings at the Step of Dwelling was just how powerful the Dwelling of Desert can be in helping us live in darkness. We learn the same truth at Birthing too, coming to know that even though we are often in darkness, and parts of ourselves are still underground, our spirituality is taking root, growing, and pushing through to life. In its own time, when the pregnancy is completed, it will emerge from hiddenness. Meanwhile, every day of our lives we can learn to feel where life is emerging from similar hiddenness.

And finally, human birth is a bearing. In spirituality this places before us the questions of what we are bearing in our spirituality. It poses the question of what we are willing to bear for the sake of Transforming ourselves and the face of the Earth. Birthing would say we bear bodiliness, enfleshment, new life; passion, emotion, and feeling; blood and water; labor and pain. Birthing would teach we bear human selves and remind us that genuine spirituality always leads in this direction too. The giving birth to our own selves and to other selves for the sake of one another is giving birth to dreams and customs and spiritualities that make life human for all the peoples of the world. Birthing would remind us that every new creation means the entire Universe must be ready to shift and make room; it makes midwives of us all. Birthing would teach, finally, that we are called to give birth to the God waiting to be born from us, that we are, in Meister Eckhart's description: "Mothers of God; for God is always needing to be born."

When that happens, the silence will be forever broken and we shall hear a rushing out, a symphonic, rustling, heart-wrenching, delight-filled sound. When that happens, we will be suffused, at least for the time being, with the celebration, festivity, and happiness of Birthing which has brought us into Transforming. As with all birthing, the moment will be unmistakable, and for a while we shall be able to forget the labor and the effort, reveling in the knowledge that genuine new life has entered the world.

And that is the direction of Transformation—and the direction of Spirituality too. A dance from listening through questioning, mourning, and bonding that issues in birthing. A dance that itself begins with Awakening and Dis-Covering, moves to Creating and Dwelling, and is impelled forward by Nourishing and Traditioning. A dance that leads to Communion with the Mystery residing at the center of all that is, and so to Communion with everyone and everything. A dance that is as yet not over and never will be.

Instead, the Step of Transforming, issuing as it does in the final moment of Birthing, now reveals itself as a beginning as well, and we realize we are called to initiate the Dance once more. We dwell in Mystery and Mystery dwells in us. We have begun the personal Transforming of our selves and our world. And in doing so, we have been reborn into a new, deeper Awakening, leading on to further Dis-Covering, Creating, and Dwelling, and still other rhythms of Nourishing and Traditioning. The Dance of the Spirit is over. The Dance of the Spirit begins.

The Practice of Transforming

Ideally, the seven practices of Transforming are opportunities not only to *do* the work of Transforming, but to enable Transforming to happen in your life. They are intended to help you make Transforming a permanent part of your spirituality. Ideally, you should practice at least one of them every day, giving yourself a full complement of fifteen or twenty minutes (which may be divided into parts, or be expanded to twice daily, or in some cases not be applicable), even if you must rearrange your day. Done consistently, as is true of the other Steps, they become rituals in your life, Nourishment for your life, ways of Traditioning to others, sources for further Awakening, Dis-Covery, and Creating. They will enable you to dwell in the center of Mystery. The preliminary steps for each practice—or in some cases the *preparation* for a practice that will be carried on later— are to:

    • Sit comfortably and easily, in a quiet place if possible, but on a bus or a train if that is necessary.

    • Shut out any outside noise by attentiveness to your inner self.

    • Close your eyes and become attuned to your breathing, to the rhythm and pace of your breath. Be sure to spend at least five minutes coming to awareness of your breathing. Inhale gently; exhale gently. Feel your body coming to a place of Dwelling. For some practices, you will need to open your eyes after the first five minutes; for others closing them is essential. You will know by now which is appropriate.

Practice 1: The Silences Within Us

Read the practice first. Then engage in the three preliminary steps.

After five minutes of rhythmic breathing, dwell with the following questions, and allow the responses to well up from your own depths.

1. What is something in yourself about which you were once silent but are silent no longer?

2. What were the circumstances that helped you move out of silence?

3. Are there any women or men who empowered you to break your silence? Have you in turn empowered others to break their silences?

4. What has happened to you personally because you are no longer silent in this area?

5. What silences in yourself remain to be broken?

6. In what ways, if any, are your own silences related to those of silent people around you?

Spend at least five minutes dwelling with your responses to these questions before concluding the practice.

Practice 2: Taking Time for Mourning*

Read the practice first. Then engage in the three preliminary steps. You may find this practice is one you want to do with one or two others or even with a larger group.

When you have become quiet, reflect on something within your life that needs to be mourned.

1. Locate that part of yourself that is aware of this need to mourn, that feels and thinks about it, and that wishes to act in relation to it. Imagine this part of yourself as if it were a character in a book. What is she like? How does she spend her time? What is important to her? Describe her as carefully and as fully as you can.

2. Locate that part of yourself that does not want to mourn, that does not want to be aware of the need, that does not want to talk or think about it. What is she like? How does she spend her time? What is important to her? Again, describe her as carefully and as completely as you can.

3. Allow these two voices within yourself to be in conversation with each other. The point is not to eliminate one or the other voice, but to hear them speaking with each other. You may want to (a) write down the conversation, (b) describe it to someone else in the group, (c) role-play the characters within yourself. If you are in a group, you may wish to hear from each person.

4. Finally, decide on one step you will take in order to move through the mourning process, and ask the group for whatever help you may need.

Alternate Practices: Choose a social or public issue (nuclear war, the battering of women, unemployment) and hold a similar conversation.

*Adapted from the work of Mary Watkins.

Practice 3: Our Experiences of Bonding

Read the practice first. Then engage in the three preliminary steps. Like practice 2, this one may be more fruitful if done with others, because our experiences can both nourish and empower one another.

1. Choose an image or symbol of Bonding as it has occurred in your life thus far.
   (Share these images and symbols if you are in a group.)

2. When are three times you bonded with other girls before you were fifteen?

   _____

   _____

   _____

3. When are three times you as an adult bonded with other women?

   _____

   _____

   _____

4. What did you *receive* from these bondings?

5. What did you *give* in these bondings?

6. What conclusions and resolutions does your experience of bonding lead you to make now, and for the future?

Practice 4: The Experience of Birth

Read the practice first. Then engage in the three preliminary steps.

Your task during this day is to reflect on the experience of birth from one of four perspectives (or on all four for four different days, if you wish).

1. Go through your house or your apartment and find ten things that symbolize birth for you (your children, a dress that did not fit you but does now, an egg . . .). Then go outside, or if you are out for the day, find ten things that symbolize birth for you in the wider society. What do they tell you of the Birth of your own spirituality?

2. Call or write to someone you know who is pregnant or who has recently given birth, and ask her to tell you about it. When you have finished the conversation, try to dis-cover what the conversation has told you about the birth of your own spirituality.

3. Call or write to someone with whom you have a relationship being born. Can you make any connections between this friendship and the birth of your own spirituality?

4. Examine your life over the past year, and choose at least three experiences of birth that you can recall. What is their relation to the birth of your Spirituality?

Practice 5: Naming Ourselves Before God

Read the practice first. Then engage in the three preliminary steps.

Having danced the Steps of our Spirituality, it is time for us to choose our own names before God. They may be our own names, just as they are. But they may also be names we wish to be known by in our Presence before God, such as "She who calls upon you," "She who is friend to the universe," "She who is needy," etc. They may be names by which we wish to be known before God only for this one day, or they may be names we are choosing for the indefinite future.

But the point is, we choose our names ourselves. And then we use that name as a mantra, repeating it gently and slowly with our breath as we place ourselves in the presence of Mystery.

Repeat your name now, slowly and with great reverence:

After repeating your name slowly, listen for your name spoken back to you: by Thou, by other people, by the universe.

Let the sound of your name, spoken to you during the day, remind you that you are always in the presence of Mystery.

Conclude the practice with five minutes of silent breathing.

Practice 6: Naming Our God

Read the practice first. Then engage in the three preliminary steps.

Having moved through the Seven Steps of Spirituality, we now come to the moment where we choose to give a name or to give *no* name to the Mystery in whose presence we dwell. That Mystery has many names: Some are very familiar, such as God, Father, Holy Spirit; others are less familiar, such as Goddess, Mother, Lady Wisdom, Thou. Still others may be very private and personal, known only to the Holy and ourselves, while others of us may choose not to name God at all, but simply to be in the presence of Mystery. This practice is one where we address God, either by using a particular Name (for the One who is beyond all names) or by addressing the Holy by offering our complete silence.

Begin by placing yourself gently in the presence of Mystery.

Believe yourself cherished, embraced, gifted, loved, and received.

In the center of this relationship, speak the name: once or rhythmically in repetition, or simply by letting your breath be your speaking.

Now allow yourself not only to listen but to hear all of Creation bonding with you in speaking this name.

Conclude by rhythmic breathing for at least five minutes.

Practice 7: The Vision of Transforming*

Read the practice first. Then engage in the three preliminary steps.

The following prayer is an appropriate ending to these practices and to these Steps. It can be used by a woman alone, by a group praying its spirituality together, or as part of a ritual of celebration. It can be taught to our children, presented as a choral reading, or given as a gift. For now, however, it is enough that having Awakened to, Dis-Covered, and Created the forms by which we Dwell in Mystery, we enter this prayer as a source of Nourishing, Traditioning, and Transforming. For it is an embodiment and an incarnation of all the Steps. It is also an embodiment and an incarnation of what our Spirituality is now and may be in the future.

> And then all that has divided us will merge
> And then compassion will be wedded to power
> And then softness will come to a world that is harsh and unkind
> And then both men and women will be gentle
> And then both women and men will be strong
> And then no person will be subject to another's will
> And then all will be rich and free and varied
> And then the greed of some will give way to the needs of many
> And then all will share equally in the Earth's abundance
> And then all will care for the sick and the weak and the old
> And then all will nourish the young
> And then all will cherish life's creatures
> And then all will live in harmony with each other and the Earth
> And then everywhere will be called Eden once again.

*From Judy Chicago, *The Dinner Party* (Garden City: Doubleday & Co., 1979), p. 256.

Epilogue
A Benediction

When a religious ritual is coming to a conclusion, most people throughout our world do not separate until they have received a blessing from one another. This happens as well in the more ordinary rituals of our daily lives where mothers bless daughters when they are parting, children bless parents, friends wish a blessing on friends. "Go with God," we say, or "Be well." It may even happen that the blessing is in a form where we ask the other not only to receive a blessing but to become a blessing too.

So it is with us now. We have not danced the *Dance of the Spirit* alone. Instead, we have engaged in its movements with the great company of women preceding us in the past, Mechtild and Julian, Esther and Sara. We have also partnered one another as women of the same time, coming into a simultaneous awakening, dis-covering, creating, dwelling, and nourishing. And we have danced toward the next generations too, even those not yet born, as we offered traditioning and transforming. Finally, we have danced with and in and through the power of the Great Spirit, the Mystery, Thou.

As we come to this resting point, it is fitting to offer benediction for ourselves and all those others that the dance might continue. As we pause both to give and receive blessing, let us imagine the voices of millions chanting with love and tenderness as well as with a power that crosses continents and centuries. Let us imagine a benediction that goes beyond race and religion. Let us imagine a benediction between poor and wealthy, weak and strong, weary and well rested. And let us pray the benediction heals and restores a bruised, broken, and battered world as we sing:

> May the Spirit of the Dance be with you.
> May the Spirit of Awakening touch you, that you
> in turn may touch one another, in your celebrations and your
> woundedness, in your going out and your return.
> May the Spirit of Dis-Covering find you, that
> you in turn may find one another, in your listening and
> remembering, in your brokenness and your connection.
> May the Spirit of Creating fashion you, that you
> in turn may fashion one another, in sensitivity and in gentleness,
> in artistry and awe.
> May the Spirit of Dwelling quiet you, that you
> in turn may be quiet resting places for one another, in the
> desert and the garden, in the city and at home.
> May the Spirit of Nourishing feed you, that you
> in turn may feed one another, in your hungers and your yearnings,
> in your neediness and your losses.
> May the Spirit of Traditioning inspire you, that
> you in turn may inspire one another, as lovers and teachers,
> as mentors and models.
> May the Spirit of Transforming re-create you, that
> you in turn may give new life to one another, and to all of
> Earth's creatures, and to the Earth itself.

Notes

Chapter 1

p. 4. In *Mysticism* (1911; reprint, New York: E.P. Dutton, 1961), pp. 176ff., Evelyn Underwood describes Awakening as the first step in the mystical life. Contemporary women writing on awakening include Carol Ochs, *Women and Spirituality* (Totowa, N.J.: Rowman and Allanheld, 1983), who on pp. 124–27 reinterprets Underwood's Awakening; and Carol Christ, *Diving Deep and Surfacing: Women Writers on Spiritual Quest* (Boston: Beacon Press, 1980), who describes a sequence of moving from nothingness to awakening to insight to new naming. See also Kate Chopin, *The Awakening*, edited by Margaret Cully (1911; reprint, New York: W.W. Norton, 1977).

p. 6. See *Breakthrough: Meister Eckhart's Creation Spirituality in New Translation*, with an introduction and commentaries by Matthew Fox (Garden City: Doubleday & Co., 1980). See esp. sermon 8, "This Is Spirituality: Waking Up," pp. 126–36, and sermon 9, "Waking Up to the Nearness of God's Kingdom," pp. 137–50.

p. 10. Her relation with Agnes Whistling Elk is described in Lynn Andrews, *Medicine Woman* (San Francisco: Harper & Row, 1983); *Jaguar Woman* (San Francisco: Harper & Row, 1985); and *Crystal Woman* (New York: Warner Books, 1987), among others.

p. 12. These quotations are taken from records of people reflecting on religious and mystical experiences that have occurred to them. Timothy Beardsworth, *A Sense of Presence* (Manchester College, Oxford: Religious Experience Research Unit, 1977), pp. 18, 55, 58–59.

p. 13. Edward Robinson, *The Original Vision. A Study of the Religious Experience of Childhood* (New York: Seabury Press, 1983), p. 51.

p. 14. Ntozake Shange, *for colored girls who have considered suicide when the rainbow is enuf* (New York: Macmillan, 1977), p.63.

p. 14. The phrase about the world "splitting open" is from Muriel Rukeyser's poem on Käthe Kollwitz. See Muriel Rukeyser, "Käthe Kollwitz," in Muriel Rukeyser, *The Speed of Darkness* (New York: Random House, 1968), p. 103.

p. 14. These quotations are taken from Mary Field Belenky et al., *Women's Ways of Knowing* (New York: Basic Books, Inc., 1986), pp. 73, 85.

p. 15. The book is Karen Petersen and J. J. Wilson, *Women Artists. Recognition and Reappraisal from the Early Middle Ages to the Twentieth Century* (New York: Harper & Row, 1976).

p. 17. Elizabeth Janeway, *Powers of the Weak* (New York: Knopf, 1980), pp. 157, 161–85.

pp. 18–19. Robinson, *op. cit.*, pp. 159–60.

Chapter 2

pp. 29–30. Two women who have given serious attention to *The Divine Comedy* are Helen Luke and Dorothy Sayers. See Helen Luke, *Dark Wood to White Rose: A Study of Meanings in Dante's Divine Comedy* (New Mexico: Dove Publications, 1975); and Dorothy Sayers, *The Comedy of Dante Alighieri*, 3 vols. (London/ Baltimore: Penguin, 1949, 1955, 1962), *Hell, Purgatory, Paradise* (with Barbara Reynolds).

p. 31. Timothy Beardsworth, *A Sense of Presence* (Manchester College, Oxford: Religious Experience Research Unit, 1977), p. 90. The woman writing this was seventy-four at the time. The sense of Presence is also described at length by William James, *Varieties of Religious Experience*, the Gifford Lectures of 1901–2 (New York: New American Library, 1958), pp. 61–65.

p. 31. Beardsworth, *Presence*, p. 121.

p. 32. The Book of Ruth is often thought to be a love story between Ruth and her kinsman, Boaz. It is a love story, but far more centrally the story of the love of Ruth and Naomi. For contemporary biblical scholarship on the Book of Ruth, see Phyllis Trible, *God and the Rhetoric of Sexuality* (Philadelphia: Fortress Press, 1978), pp. 166–99.

p. 33. Simone Weil, *Waiting for God* (New York: Harper Colophon Books, 1951); and Etty Hillesum, *An Interrupted Life: The Diaries of Etty Hillesum 1941–43* (New York: Pantheon Books, Inc., 1983).

p. 33. David Hay, *Exploring Inner Space* (New York: Penguin Books, 1982), pp. 133–34. Hay does not use the same framework I am using here, but the expression of the experience is the same.

p. 34. See T. S. Eliot, *Four Quartets: The Dry Salvages* (1943; reprint, New York: Harcourt Brace Jovanovich, 1971), p. 44.

p. 34. Beardsworth, *Presence,* p. 48.

p. 34. Ibid., p. 83.

p. 35. See Elizabeth Barrett Browning, *Sonnets from the Portuguese and Other Love Poems* (New York: Doubleday & Co., 1954).

pp. 35–36. See Bruno Bettelheim, *The Uses of Enchantment* (New York: Vintage, 1977).

pp. 37–38. The following section draws on and works with the seminal book of Jean Baker Miller, *Toward a New Psychology of Women,* 2nd ed. (Boston: Beacon Press, 1986). See chapter 4, "Strengths," pp. 29ff. Miller works as visiting scholar in residence at the Stone Center, Wellesley College, Wellesley, Massachusetts, exploring issues critical in the lives of women.

pp. 39–40. The woman who has developed this most eloquently is Nel Noddings in her *Caring* (Berkeley: University of California Press, 1984). See also Carol Gilligan, *In a Different Voice* (Cambridge: Harvard University Press, 1982).

p. 40. The woman who has taught us most about women as essentially "connected" is Nancy Chodorow in her *The Reproduction of Mothering* (Berkeley: University of California Press, 1978). See also Gilligan, *Different Voice.*

p. 42. Mechtild, quoted in Matthew Fox, *Original Blessing* (San Francisco: Bear and Co., 1983), p. 69. Mechtild was the first mystic to write in German and her book *The Flowing Light of the Godhead* is famous for its mystical bridal poetry after the Song of Songs. Among her many images for spirituality are dancing, sinking, growth, awakening, compassion, and letting go. Her work deeply influenced the great medieval mystic Meister Eckhart. See *Breakthrough: Meister Eckhart's Creation Spirituality in New Translation with Introduction and Commentaries by Matthew Fox* (Garden City: Doubleday & Co., 1980), p. 36.

p. 42. Virginia Woolf, *A Room of One's Own* (1929; reprint, New York: Harcourt Brace Jovanovich, 1957), p. 108.

p. 42. Hildegard of Bingen (1098–1179) is the twelfth-century woman we know as an author of visionary works, composer, prophetess and abbess, and teacher. Music was central in her spirituality. See Hildegard of Bingen, *Scivias,* trans. Bruce Hozeski (San Francisco: Bear and Co., 1986). "*Scivias*" means "know thy ways." See also *Illuminations of Hildegard of Bingen*, Text by Hildegard of Bingen with Commentary by Matthew Fox (Santa Fe: Bear and Co., 1985).

Julian of Norwich (1342–1420) was unknown until this century. Today she is the most widely read and influential mystic of the English spiritual tradition. She has influenced writers as diverse as Annie Dillard, who calls her "Julie Norwich," and T. S. Eliot, who as a result of including it in the climax of *Four Quartets* has made her most famous line, "All shall be well; and all manner of thing shall be well," the triumph of hope and love. See Gloria Durka, *Praying with Julian of Norwich* (Winona, Minn: St. Mary's Press, 1989).

p. 42. For extended treatment of Beruriah and Bertha Pappenheim, see Elizabeth Koltun, ed., *The Jewish Woman: New Perspectives* (New York: Schocken Books, Inc., 1976), pp. 149–63, 261–71.

p. 42. For further descriptions of the African goddesses, see Sabrina Sojourner, "From the House of Yemanja: The Goddess Heritage of Black Women," in Charlene Spretnak, ed., *The Politics of Women's Spirituality* (Garden City: Doubleday & Co., 1982), pp. 57–63.

p. 43. Sara and Hagar are the wife and the concubine of the patriarch Abraham. See Phyllis Trible, *Texts of Terror* (Philadelphia: Fortress Press, 1984) for their story.

p. 43. Esther followed Vashti as the wife of King Ahasuerus when the latter refused to display her beauty before the king and his friends. See Mary Gendler, "The Restoration of Vashti," in Koltun, *Jewish Woman*, pp. 241–47.

p. 43. The relation between Medusa and Athena is described in Catherine Keller, *From a Broken Web: Separation, Sexism and Self* (Boston: Beacon Press, 1986), pp. 67ff.

p. 44. Annie Dillard calls God "Holy the Firm" in her book of the same name (New York: Bantam Books, 1979), pp. 3–4.

p. 46. *The Cloud of Unknowing* is a classic of medieval English spirituality. For a modern edition, see *The Cloud of Unknowing*, edited with an introduction by James Walsh (New York: Paulist Press, 1981). Walsh agrees that the most definitive text is still Dr. Phyllis Hodgson, ed., *The Cloud of Unknowing* (New York/London: Early English Text Society, 1944).

p. 47. Edna St. Vincent Millay, "Dirge Without Music," in *The Mentor Book of Major American Poets*, ed. Oscar Williams and Edwin Honig (New York: New American Library, 1962), p. 419.

Chapter 3

p. 59. *Illuminations of Hildegard of Bingen* (Santa Fe: Bear and Co., 1985), p. 116.

p. 59. T. S. Eliot, "The Dry Salvages," from *Four Quartets* (New York: Harcourt, Brace, Jovanovich, 1971), p. 44.

p. 60. Suzanne Langer says, "Art is the creation of perceptible form, expressive of human feeling," in *Problems of Art* (New York: Charles Scribner's Sons, 1957), p. 80.

p. 61. These lines are from Gerard Manley Hopkins, "God's Grandeur."

p. 63. J. D. Salinger, *Raise High the Roof Beam, Carpenters and Seymour, an Introduction* (Boston: Little, Brown, 1959), p. 236.

p. 64. For application of these steps to teaching, see Maria Harris, *Teaching and Religious Imagination* (San Francisco: Harper & Row, 1987).

p. 64–65. Annie Dillard, *Pilgrim at Tinker Creek* (New York: Bantam Books, 1974), pp. 15–16.

p. 67. Anne Sexton, "Not So. Not So," in Anne Sexton, *The Awful Rowing Toward God* (Boston: Houghton Mifflin, 1975), p. 83.

pp. 67–68. This interview is recorded in Mary Field Belenky et al., *Women's Ways of Knowing* (New York: Basic Books, Inc., 1986), p. 99.

pp. 68–69. This story is found in Robert Samples, *The Metaphoric Mind* (Reading: Addison-Wesley, 1975), p. 91.

p. 71. Alice Walker, *The Color Purple* (New York: Washington Square Press, 1982), p. 247.

p. 75. Sexton, "The Rowing Endeth," from Sexton, *Awful Rowing*, p. 85.

Chapter 4

pp. 90–91. Thich Nhat Hanh, *The Miracle of Mindfulness* (Boston: Beacon Press, 1976), p. 4.

pp. 92–93. A classic work on Sabbath is Abraham Heschel, *The Sabbath* (New York: Noonday Press, 1959). There is, of course, more to Sabbath than rest, such as re-creation in community, but at this step, the aspect of rest is paramount. See also Theresa Sallnow, "Sinai in the Inner City. Rediscovering the Desert in Contemporary Spirituality," in *British Journal of Religious Education*, 8, 1 (Autumn, 1985), pp. 9–12.

p. 96. See Marge Piercy's poem, "The common living dirt," in her *Stone, Paper, Knife* (New York: Knopf, 1983), pp. 123–24.

p. 96. From *Pilgrim at Tinker Creek* (New York: Bantam Books, 1974), p. 248.

p. 97. Septuagenarian May Sarton speaks of autumn, crocuses, lavender asters, and orange maples, in *Journal of a Solitude* (New York: W.W. Norton, 1977), p. 206.

pp. 100–01. Kathryn Allen Rabuzzi, *The Sacred and the Feminine* (New York: Seabury Press, 1982), esp. pp. 98, 125.

p. 102. Etty Hillesum, *An Interrupted Life: The Diaries of Etty Hillesum 1941–43* (New York: Pantheon Books, Inc., 1983), p. 176.

Chapter 5

pp. 118–119. This prayer, by Catherine A. Callaghan, is found in Linda Clark, Marian Ronan, and Eleanor Walker, *Image Breaking—Image Building* (New York: Pilgrim Press, 1981), p. 61.

p. 119. Roger Rosenblatt, *Children of War* (Garden City: Anchor Press/Doubleday), 1982.

p. 119. Anthony de Mello, *Sadhana: A Way to God* (Garden City: Doubleday Image, 1984), pp. 3–4.

p. 120. See M. Basil Pennington, *Centering Prayer* (Garden City: Image Books, 1982).

pp. 121–122. Margaret Miles, *Fullness of Life: Foundations for a New Asceticism* (Philadelphia: Westminster Press, 1981), pp. 150–60.

p. 123. Judy Chicago, *The Dinner Party* (Garden City: Doubleday & Co., 1979).

p. 123. Janet Kalven and Mary Buckley, eds., *Women's Spirit Bonding* (New York: Pilgrim Press, 1984), pp. 353–55.

p. 123. In an unpublished course paper of Christina Braudaway-Bauman, "Rituals in Our Lives" (Boston: Women's Theological Center, May, 1985).

p. 124. Many of the rituals named on this page are found in Clark et al., *Image Breaking*, pp. 48–60.

p. 124. The rituals by Wenig, Janowitz, Cantor, and Plaskow are found in Carol Christ and Judith Plaskow, eds., *Womanspirit Rising* (San Francisco: Harper & Row, 1979), pp. 174–92.

p. 125. Rosemary Radford Ruether, *Women-Church: Theology and Practice of Feminist Liturgical Communities* (San Francisco: Harper & Row, 1985).

p. 126. Other approaches to ritual in women's lives can be found in Diane Mariechild, *Mother Wit* (Trumansburg, N.Y.: Crossing Press, 1981); and in the work of two centers: the Center for Women and Religion, 2465 Le Conte Avenue, Berkeley, Calif. 94709; and W.A.T.E.R. (Women's Alliance for Theology, Ethics and Ritual), 8035 Thirteenth Street, Silver Spring, Md. 20910.

p. 127. Abraham Heschel, *The Prophets* (New York: Harper & Row, 1962), p. 5.

p. 127. Molly Rush, "Living, Mothering, Resisting," *Christianity and Crisis*, Volume 40 (December 8, 1980), p. 348; and Liane Ellison Norman, "Living Up to Molly," ibid., pp. 341–44.

pp. 127–28. John Simpson and Jana Bennett, *The Disappeared and the Mothers of the Plaza: The Story of the 11,000 Argentinians Who Vanished* (New York: St. Martin's Press, 1985).

p. 128. Eleanor Coerr, *Sadako and the Thousand Paper Cranes* (New York: Dell Publishing Co., 1977).

p. 129. Ruether, *Women-Church*, pp. 233–34.

pp. 130–131. The work of Elisabeth Kübler-Ross forms the basis for the healing of memories found in Dennis Linn and Matthew Linn, *Healing Life's Hurts: Healing Memories Through the Five Stages of Forgiveness* (Ramsey, N.J.: Paulist Press, 1978).

pp. 131–32. For the meanings of justice given here, see John R. Donahue, "Biblical Perspectives on Justice," in *The Faith That Does Justice*, ed. John C. Haughey (New York: Paulist Press, 1977); Matthew Fox, *A Spirituality Named Compassion* (Minneapolis: Winston Press, 1979); and Walter Brueggemann, "Voices of the Night—Against Justice," in Walter Brueggemann, Sharon Parks, and Thomas H. Groome, *To Act Justly, Love Tenderly, Walk Humbly* (New York: Paulist Press, 1986), pp. 5–28.

p. 133. Adapted from the ten commandments of justice of Arthur Jones in *National Catholic Reporter*, July 6, 1984, p. 5.

Chapter 6

p. 147. Erik Erikson, *Childhood and Society* (New York: W.W. Norton, 1963); and Erik Erikson and Joan Erikson, "On Generativity and Identity," in *Harvard Educational Review* 51 (May 1981), pp. 249–69.

pp. 148–49. Maya Angelou, *I Know Why the Caged Bird Sings* (New York: Random House, 1969), pp. 90–98.

pp. 149–51. On teaching, see Maria Harris, *Teaching and Religious Imagination* (San Francisco: Harper & Row, 1987).

pp. 151–52. On mentoring, see Sharan Merriam, "Mentors and Protégés: A Critical Review of the Literature," *Adult Education Quarterly* 33, no. 3 (Spring 1983), pp. 161–73; and Margaret Hennig and Anne Jardim, *The Managerial Woman* (Garden City: Anchor/Doubleday, 1977).

p. 152. Lynn Andrews, *Medicine Woman* (San Francisco: Harper & Row, 1983), p. 133.

p. 154. Edward Robinson, *The Original Vision* (New York: Seabury Press, 1983), pp. 28, 65–66, 71.

p. 156. Merlin Stone, *When God Was a Woman* (New York: Harcourt Brace Jovanovich/Dial Press, 1976), pp. 4, 53, 195.

p. 156. See Gloria Steinem and G. Chesler, *Wonder Woman, A Ms book* (New York: Holt, Rinehart & Winston/Warner Books, 1974).

p. 156. Letty Cottin Pogrebin, "Going Public As a Jew," *Ms.* (July-August 1987), p. 195.

pp. 159–160. Rosemary Cingari, in an unpublished paper entitled "Lost, Broken or Hidden Images."

pp. 161–162. Gabriel Moran, *Religious Education Development* (Minneapolis: Winston Press, 1983), develops these rhythms in chs. 7, 8, and 9.

p. 162. May Sarton, *Mrs. Stevens Hears the Mermaids Singing* (New York: W.W. Norton, 1965), p. 183.

pp. 162–163. Elise Boulding, *Children and Solitude* (Wallingford, Pa.: Pendle Hill, 1962), pp. 20–21.

p. 169. Adapted from Mary Terese Donze, *In My Heart Room* (Liguori, Mo.: Liguori Publications, 1982).

pp. 175–78. Practices 6 and 7 are adapted from Aileen A. Doyle, *Youth Retreats: Creating Sacred Space for Young People* (Winona, Minn.: St. Mary's Press, 1986).

Chapter 7

pp. 180–81. The book of the Bible called Genesis tells Sara's story, especially in chapters 17–21. Hannah's song is found in the First Book of Samuel, chapter 2. Mary's canticle called the Magnificat is in the Gospel of Luke, chapter 1.

p. 181. See Phyllis Trible, *Texts of Terror* (Philadelphia: Fortress Press, 1984), for the stories of these three women as they meet us today.

p. 181. Ruth and Naomi are met in the Bible in the Book of Ruth. Miriam's story is found in Exodus, especially in chapters 2 and 15. The stories of Esther and Vashti are told in the Book of Esther: Vashti, first wife of King Ahasuerus, refused to come into his presence when he wished to display her beauty; Esther opposed the king's chief steward, Haman, who wished to destroy the Jews. Mary Magdalene is met throughout the New Testament and was the first to know of the Resurrection of Jesus from the dead.

p. 182. Tillie Olsen, *Silences* (New York: Delacorte Press, 1978); Adrienne Rich, *Of Lies, Secrets and Silence* (New York: W.W. Norton, 1979); Nancy A. Falk and Rita M. Gross, eds., *Unspoken Worlds: Women's Religious Lives in Non-Western Cultures* (San Francisco: Harper & Row, 1980); Jane Roland Martin, *Reclaiming a Conversation* (New Haven: Yale University Press, 1985); and Alicia Ostriker, *Stealing the Language* (Boston: Beacon Press, 1987).

p. 182. Mary Field Belenky et al., *Women's Ways of Knowing* (New York: Basic Books, Inc., 1986), p. 18, elaborates on this point through the study of the lives of over one hundred women, commenting in their own words on this aspect of their lives.

p. 182. In *Pintig: Lifepulse in Cold Steel* (Kowloon, Hong Kong: Resource Center for Philippine Concerns, 1979), p. 118.

pp. 182–83. Terrors visited on women are described in Mary Daly, *Gyn/Ecology: The Metaethics of Radical Feminism* (Boston: Beacon Press, 1978), who quotes David and Vera Mace on Hindu suttee, p. 124; and Andrea Dworkin, *Woman Hating: A Radical Look at Sexuality* (New York: E.P. Dutton, 1976).

p. 184. Margaret Atwood, *Surfacing* (New York: Simon & Schuster, 1972), pp. 222–23.

p. 185. "Hearing one another into speech" is a phrase from the work of Nelle Morton. See her *The Journey Is Home* (Boston: Beacon Press, 1986).

p. 188. Erich Lindemann, "Symptomatology and Management of Acute Grief," in Robert Fulton, ed., *Death and Identity* (New York: John Wiley and Sons, 1965), pp. 186–201; and Elisabeth Kübler-Ross, *On Death and Dying* (New York: Macmillan, 1969).

p. 190. For the stories of such women as the Pankhursts, the Grimkes, Sojourner Truth, Susan B. Anthony, Elizabeth Cady Stanton, Margaret Mead, and others, see Dale Spender, *Women of Ideas* (Boston: Routledge & Kegan Paul, 1982).

p. 190. Singers and novelists cited here are Judy Collins, "Bread and Roses," on *The First Fifteen Years* (Los Angeles: Elektra/Asylum Records, 1977); Holly Near and Ronnie Gilbert, "Singing for our Lives," on *Lifeline* (Oakland: Redwood Records, 1983); Cris Williamson, "Sister" on *The Changer and the Changed* (Oakland: Olivia Records, 1975); Jane Austen, *Pride and Prejudice* (New York: Bantam Books, 1981); Louisa May Alcott, *Little Women* (Boston: Little, Brown, 1968), cent. ed.; Alice Walker, *The Color Purple* (New York: Washington Square Press, 1982); Mary Gordon, *Final Payments* (New York: Random House, 1978), and *The Company of Women* (New York: Random House, 1980).

p. 193. Ina Gaskin, *Spiritual Midwifery* (Summertown, Tenn.: The Book Publishing Co., 1977), p. 282.

pp. 193–94. Charlotte Perkins Gilman, *His Religion and Hers* (New York: Century, 1923).

p. 198. Mary Watkins teaches how to engage in this exercise in "Moral Imagination and Peace Activism: Discerning the Inner Voices," *Psychological Perspectives: A Semi-Annual Review of Jungian Thought* (Spring 1985), pp. 77–93.

p. 203. Judy Chicago, *The Dinner Party* (Garden City: Doubleday & Co., 1979), p. 256.

p. 204. Cited in Matthew Fox, *Original Blessing* (Santa Fe: Bear and Co., 1986), p. 222.

Index

INDEX

INDEX

The author expresses gratitude to the following for granting permission to quote from their work:

Excerpts from *The Dinner Party* by Judy Chicago. Copyright © 1979 by Judy Chicago. Reprinted by permission of Doubleday, a division of Bantam, Doubleday, Dell Publishing Group, Inc.

To Catherine Callaghan for use of her prayer "To The Goddess" used by permission of the publisher from *Image-Breaking/Image-Building: A Handbook for Creative Worship with Women of Christian Tradition*, by Linda Clark, Marian Ronan and Eleanor Walker. Copyright 1981, The Pilgrim Press, New York, New York.

To St. Mary's Press, Winona, Minnesota, for permission to adapt the workshop-handout "Strength-Weakness Statements for Dyads." Adapted from *Youth Retreats: Creating Sacred Space for Young People*, by Aileen A. Doyle (Winona, Minn.: St. Mary's Press, 1986). Used by permission of the publisher.

To Faber and Faber, Limited to quote from "The Dry Salvages" in *Four Quartets* by T.S. Eliot.

To David Higham Associates Limited and Penguin Books, Publishers, for permission to use Dorothy L. Sayers's translation of lines from *The Comedy of Dante Alighieri*.

To Macmillan Publishing Company for permission to quote from *For Colored Girls Who Have Considered Suicide When the Rainbow Is Enuf* by Ntozake Shange. Copyright © 1975, 1976, 1977 by Ntozake Shange.

To Carla De Sola for adaptation of her work in *Learning Through Dance*. (New York: Paulist Press, 1974).

The Bible text in this publication (except for the Psalms) is from the Revised Standard Version of the Bible, copyrighted 1946, 1952, 1971 by the Division of Christian Education of the National Council of the Churches of Christ in the U.S.A. and used by permission.

The psalms quoted in this book are from *Psalms Anew: In Inclusive Language*, compiled by Nancy Schreck and Maureen Leach. (Winona, Minn.: Saint Mary's Press, 1986). Used by permission of the publisher. All rights reserved.